Choma
A Boy of Central Africa

By
Ella M. Robinson

TEACH Services, Inc.
P U B L I S H I N G
www.TEACHServices.com • (800) 367-1844

World rights reserved. This book or any portion thereof may not be copied or reproduced in any form or manner whatever, except as provided by law, without the written permission of the publisher, except by a reviewer who may quote brief passages in a review.

This book was written to provide truthful information in regard to the subject matter covered. The author assumes full responsibility for the accuracy of all facts and quotations as cited in this book. The opinions expressed in this book are the author's personal views and interpretation of the Bible, Spirit of Prophecy, and/or contemporary authors and do not necessarily reflect those of TEACH Services, Inc.

This book is sold with the understanding that the publisher is not engaged in giving spiritual, legal, medical, or other professional advice. If authoritative advice is needed, the reader should seek the counsel of a competent professional.

Copyright © 2013 TEACH Services, Inc.
ISBN-13: 978-1-4796-0214-8 (Paperback)
ISBN-13: 978-1-4796-0215-5 (ePub)
ISBN-13: 978-1-4796-0216-2 (Kindle/Mobi)

Library of Congress Control Number: 2013940327

Published by

www.TEACHServices.com • (800) 367-1844

Table of Contents

I. Choma at Home
1. Baby Luwo 7
2. The Evening Meal 9
3. Evening in the Village 11
4. Malambo's Story 13
5. Going to the Dentist 15
6. The Boiling-Water Test 17
7. A Lion Kill 19
8. A Quarrel 21
9. Planting Time 24
10. Praying for Rain 26
11. Seeking Food 28
12. The Witch Doctor 30
13. The Medicine Doctor 32

II. The Dance
14. Getting Ready 33
15. The Greetings 35
16. The Dance 37
17. The Slave Raid 40
18. Hiding 42
19. After the Raid 43
20. The Unlucky Baby 45
21. Mianda 47
22. Accused and Killed 48
23. The Legend 49

III. The Missionary's Visit

24. Oleta at Home 50
25. Getting Ready for a Trip 53
26. The Journey 55
27. At the Village 57
28. Going to School in Africa 59
29. The Meeting 62
30. At Malambo's Village 64
31. Oleta Goes Visiting 66
32. Work in the Village 69
33. Grandma's Question Answered 71
34. Choma Goes to the Mission 73

IV. Experiences at the Mission

35. Home Again 75
36. Choma's First Night 77
37. Choma's First Day 78
38. Choma's First Sabbath 80
39. Choma in Trouble 82
40. Choma Acquires Property 84
41. In the Kitchen 85
42. Tempted 87
43. The Meeting Camp 89
44. Choma Visits His Home 92
45. Daily Program of the Camp 94
46. Choma Gives Presents 96

V. Two Runaways
- 47. Queer Fears and Fancies 98
- 48. Gathering and Storing Food.. 100
- 49. Intruders.. 103
- 50. Setupa's Wedding 105
- 51. Good News... 107
- 52. Eavesdropping 109
- 53. The Plot.. 111
- 54. Taking Flight 113
- 55. Dangers 116
- 56. More Dangers 118
- 57. No Room 120

VI. Ready for Work
- 58. Charms 122
- 59. Mapepe Dies.. 124
- 60. The Burial Feast 126
- 61. Discovered... 127
- 62. Finding the Lobola 130
- 63. A Christian Wedding.. 133
- 64. Ready for Work.. 135
- 65. Building the Schoolhouse 137
- 66. One More Gleam of Light.. 140

Choma lived in a village like this

Choma at Home
1
Baby Luwo

Choma and his sister sat under a wild fig tree, arranging the clay oxen that they had just finished molding. Their herd included many kinds. Some were fat and well-favored, while others were so thin that they made one think of famine times. There were long-horned oxen, and others with short, stumpy horns. There were calves, some with pigs' tails, and some with sheep's tails. And there were herd boys that looked like cooky men. They were all finished now, and standing in the sun to dry.

Choma got up and went into the hut, leaving Nzala alone with their herd of cattle. "I die of thirst," he said, taking from a wooden peg in the wall a gourd-shell calabash of water. He drank, then unrolled his mat and lay down on the floor to sleep.

Malambo, their father, sat at the door of the hut, smoking his long reed pipe. After a time he also went inside and slept.

Mother came out of the hut. She unfastened the *ingubo* (baby-blanket) of buckskin from her back, and lifted out the baby. Then she put baby, blanket and all, on sister's back, and tied the leather thongs by which it was fastened securely around the little girl's body, under her arms and about her waist. Baby Luwo's little head bobbed about from side to side as sister hopped around on the ground.

Luwo was a happy baby. When out of the baby blanket, he rolled around on the floor of the hut, or in the yard outside. He gurgled, and cooed, and played with his toes, or with the string of beads around his waist. How he would laugh at the clink, clink, clink of the brass bangles on his arms!

Three little wooden blocks dangled from one wrist by tiny strips of leather. They had been cut from the roots of a medicine tree; and were supposed to protect the baby from harm and to make him grow fat and strong.

Today Luwo cried. The wind was dry and hot, and the flies kept biting his eyes. And he was so very thirsty. His mother had gone away to gather firewood; and no one knew that water was good for babies to drink. So Nzala could do nothing to soothe him except to rock her body gently to and fro, while she finished putting a roof on a tiny clay hut she was making.

It was a case of -

> Rock-a-by baby on sister's back,
> Dear little baby, so soft and black!

At last the crying ceased; baby was asleep. Nzala laid him on the ground and spread the baby-blanket over him. Then she stood the clay herd boys in front of the hut, and started to build a cattle-kraal of little sticks.

2
The Evening Meal

The hot air was heavy with smoke, for the tall grass around the village was being burned. It had become dry under the scorching sun, and was of little use to the cattle. They were getting thinner and thinner every day, and the cows were giving less and less milk. After the old grass was burned away, little tufts of green grass would spring up. These would keep the cattle alive until rain would come and make the pastures good again.

As the crimson sun dropped toward the east and the intense midday heat passed, the people of the village began to stir about. Malambo placed his stool outside his hut door. He sat down and filled his pipe. Two or three of his neighbors wandered over, and were invited to sit down for a chat and a smoke.

Malambo was the headman of this village, and the other men gathered where he was to talk. Today he was at the hut of Choma's mother, who was his favorite wife. She was called "Ba-ka-Milupi [mother of Milupi]," because Milupi was her oldest son. Choma had often heard his father say, "I gave many oxen for Ba-ka-Milupi. She is fair to look upon. She does much work. She does not quarrel as many women do. She is my best wife."

While the men sat and talked, mother called her little girl: "Come, Nzala, we must fetch water." She tied baby on her own back, and lifted a *nonga* (earthen waterpot) to her head. Nzala picked up her waterpot, and they started down the long path to the river. All the water holes near the village from which the women usually drew water were now dry.

The river, too, was dry. With their gourd-shell cups, they scooped a hollow in its sandy bed, and then sat down to wait for the water to seep into the hole. How good the cool sand seemed after their long walk! As soon as the hole had filled with water, they dipped it into their waterpots.

Other women and children came to the river to dig for water. They sat and talked, while the babies rolled and played on the cool sand, and the boys and girls raced around with their dogs. When all the jars were full, the women tied their babies on their backs again, lifted the waterpots to their heads, and one by one filed down the long path back to the village. The thirsty children and dogs stopped for a last drink at the water holes, and then trotted along behind.

When Nzala and her mother reached the hut, they set down their waterpots and went outside to attend to the fire. They cleared away the ashes and drew the ends of the three burning logs together. Nzala pushed a wisp of grass and a few sticks between the logs, and soon they were ablaze. She

African men and boys eating supper

knocked off some of the burning embers, threw on a few short branches, arranged the fire-stones, and set on a pot of water. Into a smaller pot she put a handful of dried fish and set it to boil.

Mother brought from the hut a dish of white *mealie* (corn) meal. She stirred the meal into the boiling water in the big pot. She kept on stirring more and more meal into the pot, until the porridge was so stiff that the wooden paddle with which she was stirring stood straight up in the middle. Then, without longer cooking, she dipped the stiff porridge out into two earthen dishes, one for the men and one for the women. She divided the fish in the same way. When the porridge and fish were cool enough, she called her family: "The food is now ready. Come, eat."

"I die of hunger," said Milupi, Choma's big brother, as he sat down on the ground by one of the big bowls of porridge. Choma and his father soon joined him. Each one reached forward and broke off a piece of the stiff porridge, made a cup-shaped depression in one end, dipped it in the dish of fish, and ate it in one bite.

Grandma and mother and Nzala ate from the other dishes of porridge and fish in a group by themselves. Grandma held baby on her knees. He did not often get porridge to eat, for he was usually left during mealtime to crawl around the yard on his little fat stomach. But today he cried, so grandma picked him up and fed him little pieces of the porridge.

The meal was quickly finished. Then Nzala set the dirty pots and dishes in the corner of the hut. The dogs would lick them out and then they would not be so hard to wash—if washed at all.

3
Evening in the Village

The village lay, circle within circle, under the bright, full moon. On the outside stretched a dark ring of thatched huts, all opening into a central yard or compound. Inside this first ring was a light circle of camp fires, some dying out in their loneliness, others blazing brightly, and revealing groups of dark figures gathered around them. Within the circular compound, was another ring made of thorn brush, inclosing the cattle-kraal, which formed the heart of the village. These people do not care to have roses or carnations growing in their front yards. They cannot eat flowers. But they greatly admire the cattle, not only for their beauty, but because they furnish them with food.

In the compound, a group of children were playing "blindman's buff," very much as children play it the world around. As they had no handkerchiefs, they covered their eyes with strips of soft bark.

Another group of children, mostly young boys, were playing "spear the pumpkin." The pumpkin was rolled from one boy to another, all the children trying to throw their spears into it while it was rolling.

Some of the smaller children were having an exciting time throwing balls. They had no baseballs nor rubber balls such as American children have, for these things do not grow on trees. The one store in the vicinity, which was about half a day's journey from the village, supplied only such things as blankets, shirts, calico, beads, dishes, and celluloid bangles, made in imitation of the ivory ones that the women liked so well.

The balls that the children were using were a kind of fruit that looked like big, green oranges. But these fruits were so dry and tasteless inside that the people did not eat them except in famine times. And as the grain bins in Malambo's village still had some food in them, the fruit on the ball-tree had been left for the children to gather and use in their games.

Chatter, laughter, and singing from the groups around the camp fires mingled with the children's noise and shouting. The men smoked, while they entertained each other with stories of the olden days before the English soldiers came into the country and stopped the fighting among the tribes. Some of the women also got out their pipes. Others helped themselves to snuff from tiny gourd-shell snuff-holders fastened to their belts. Naked babies played with little piles of dust or pebbles, or rolled and tumbled about over their mothers' knees.

After a time the younger children scampered off one by one to their huts, leaving the older ones at play. "Let us go hunting," said Choma. He was usually leader of the children's sports, because Malambo, his father, was headman of the village, and his mother was the favorite wife.

The boys at play disappeared into their huts to get their spears. The older boys were the proud possessors of real spears. The younger ones used sharpened sticks. When the boys came back, suddenly they began a terrific growling and roaring, followed by a wild rush for imaginary lions and leopards that were supposed to be prowling around the village. Every shadow was searched. After much shouting and throwing of spears, the beasts of prey were captured or driven off; the game was over.

The moon had climbed high in the sky. "Let us sleep," said Choma. He joined the group around his father's fire.

"Here comes our little zebra," teased Milupi. "Take care, he will bite."

"He is only a child," added his father tantalizingly. "Can you expect that such a little one would have courage to get his teeth knocked out? When he is a man, he will have more courage."

It is a great insult to a Batonga boy or girl to be called a zebra. Milupi was taunting his little brother with being a coward because he did not yet have his front teeth knocked out as did all the older boys and men. Away back in the early days, the people of Africa chose different ways of marking their bodies, so that the various tribes could be distinguished. Some of the tribes make marks on the forehead, by slitting the skin and rubbing in char coal, which leaves a scar. Others make large holes in the lobes of the ears or in the lips. The people of one tribe file the front teeth so that they will be pointed like those of the crocodile.

It is supposed that the Batonga people admired the cattle so much that they wished to look like them, and that this is the reason why they chose as their tribal mark to remove their four upper front teeth.

Although Choma's feelings were deeply hurt, he said nothing in reply to the taunts of his brother. He went into the hut, lay down on his mat, and rolled up in his skin blanket. The men sitting around the fire were still telling stories.

Would you like to hear one of Malambo's stories? You must remember that many of the things he said about the spirits and the medicine are not true, but are only what these poor people believe before they know about God and the Bible.

4
Malambo's Story

"It was in the days when I began to carry the spear," Malambo continued after Choma had gone away, "that there was fighting in our country. The trouble was within our own tribe. The people living to the north had raided our villages and carried away our cattle. We decided to try to rescue our stolen goods, and to punish the offenders as well.

"The chief men from the villages around gathered at the *Iwanga* hut to ask counsel of the serpent that lived there. The spirit of our warrior chief, Chimuka, lived in the *Iwanga* serpent. The serpent was free to go where he liked; but he never left the hut we had built for him to go farther than the branches of an overhanging tree. Every morning we gave him his dish of porridge and milk. "Before going to fight, we wished to learn what the outcome of the battle would be.

If the *Iwanga* serpent turned red, we knew that the victory would be ours. But if he crawled up the tree, and seemed to want to get away from us, we would not venture to go to fight, for we were sure that our enemies would be too strong for us. "On this day the serpent turned red. We knew by that sign that the spirit within him would *tie our enemies,* so that they could not fight well. There was great rejoicing. The war drums were beaten in all the villages.

"Our great medicine man made medicine water, and we anointed OUT spears. He ground up the dried heart of a leopard, and sprinkled it over our food. After we had eaten, we rested and slept for a time.

"When the night was half finished, we arose and smeared our faces with ashes and white clay. Then we marched away to meet our enemies. As we walked along the path, we chewed medicine to make ourselves invisible, that we might not be seen by our enemies. Each man was talking with his 'helping spirit.' My heart was strong, for my 'helping spirit' was the uncle of my father, who had once been a brave warrior.

"While we were away from home, our women were not allowed to dance. They were forbidden to throw anything at one another, or to strike one another, lest their friends or relatives who were fighting should be speared.

"Our enemies were not expecting us so soon. We had a great victory that day, and recovered more oxen and goods than had been taken from us. But we killed few men, and we captured no slaves, for they were of our own tribe.

"In those days I was a great warrior. I have killed two men, and leopards and lions very many."

Proudly Malambo showed the scars on his arms and shoulder. "You can see that I have fought the leopard with my own hands," he said.

"In these days there is an end of all this fighting. We can keep no more slaves. The mothers and sisters of my people who were stolen away and sold for slaves have all been returned to their homes. Now our people can live in peace, without fear; but we must dig our own fields, and do all our own work."

5
Going to the Dentist

While Choma lay on his mat and thought about how he had been teased because he still had his teeth, he decided that he would go at once to the dentist and have his teeth removed. He dreaded to have it done, for he had heard the older boys tell how painful it was. But the pain would not be so hard to bear as to be called a zebra.

In the morning before it was light, while most of the people in the village were asleep, he stole quietly out of the hut. On his shoulder was a spear, which was intended as a present for the dentist. He walked boldly down the path leading to the village where the dentist lived.

It was still early in the forenoon when Choma reached the dentist's home. After greetings had been exchanged, the dentist picked up a large smooth stone and a short wedge-shaped spike, and said, "Come." They went out in front of the hut. Choma sat down on the ground. The dentist seated himself on a low stool, and gripped the boy's head firmly between his knees. Then he called two young men so that they might be - ready to hold Choma if he struggled. But Choma was determined not to be a coward. His father should have reason to be proud that he had a brave son.

The dentist did not look for an aching tooth. He had no medicine to kill pain. He took the stone and the iron spike, and went to work. He placed

African boys playing by their hut door

the spike between two of the boy's beautiful white teeth, and drove it down between the roots. Then he drove it in on the other side of the same tooth. Choma sat quite still and did not utter a sound. To have cried out would have brought upon him the ridicule of his entire village, and all his relatives and friends for miles around would have heard of it.

One, two, three knocks of the spike against the tooth, and out it came, roots and all. Then another, and another, and still one more, until four sound teeth lay on the ground. The dentist gathered them up, made a hole in the ground, and quickly buried them out of sight.

As Choma walked home he carefully covered every drop of blood that fell from his mouth. He had been told that his teeth would grow in again if another boy, whose teeth had not been taken out, should happen to be traveling along that path and should step on the blood stains. That would mean for Choma another trip to the dentist.

When the boy was safely out of sight of the dentist's village, he left the path and crept away into the bush. He sat down on a stump and wrung his hands. "I am dying! I am dying!" he moaned. But he did not die. In a few days he was quite well again, and very proud that he had had his teeth knocked out.

6
The Boiling-Water Test

Kaluwe was Choma's best friend. His mother was also one of Malambo's wives, and he lived in the same village. The two boys were together constantly. They went together to the fields to gather green herbs, which were used for relish to eat with the porridge. They took their turn together herding village cattle, and together they searched the swamps for the finest reeds to use in matmaking, and the palm forest for the most perfect fronds from which to make baskets. And many were the days that they spent in the woods digging for field mice and cooking them on camp fires made especially for the purpose.

So it was no wonder that Choma was greatly alarmed one day to hear that Kaluwe was in serious trouble. A man named Chiasa who lived in a near by village had accused him of stealing his *mealies,* or corn. The man knew well that it was not Kaluwe who had raided his corn patch. Kaluwe knew it; Choma knew it; his father and mother knew it; everybody knew it.

For years the baboons had made occasional invasions into the corn fields of this vicinity. They would some times come in large companies and steal as many ears as they could carry away. They had even been known to tie the ears of corn by the silks to their long hair, and hop away into the bush with the ears dangling about them.

But Kaluwe had been seen near Chiasa's fields about the same time that the corn was first missed. So, naturally, he was accused, and must be publicly tried.

A trial among the Batonga people at this time was not a very pleasant thing. The boiling-water test was applied. A large pot was filled with boiling medicine water, and a stone placed in the bottom of it. The accused had to put his hand into the pot and lift out the stone. If he succeeded in doing this without blistering his hand or arm, the judges decided that he was innocent. In this case, those who accused him falsely must give him a present.

If the boiling water made a blister, which usually happened, no other proof of the man's guilt was required. In the olden days, the accused man would have been sold into slavery, and the blood money given to the man whose goods he was supposed to have stolen. The only way to save a person from such a fate was for his relatives to pay a heavy ransom for him. But now the British government was settling some of the more important affairs of the country, and the selling or keeping of slaves was strictly forbidden.

Among Kaluwe's people, the penalty for theft at this time was to restore four times the value of the stolen goods.

Kaluwe was determined that he would not take the boiling-water test. But the only way he could escape it was by making a public confession that he had stolen the corn. If he did this, his fine would be made lighter, and he would not have to run the risk of being burned. Although innocent, he decided to make confession. Kaluwe's mother begged Malambo to help her son, and to settle the trouble peaceably with Chiasa.

Malambo and Milupi went with Kaluwe to see Chiasa, and offered to give him two oxen. He demanded more. There was a long *indaba* (council). The important men of both villages met to talk the matter over. Finally Chiasa agreed to take the two oxen, and the affair was settled.

7
A Lion Kill

One night a wild bellowing was heard in the cattle kraal. Men and boys and dogs came running from the surrounding huts. Some lighted torches of thatch grass, while others snatched firebrands. With these quickly made torches in one hand and spears in the other; they rushed toward the cattle-kraal. The bravest and most experienced hunters were in the lead, each man eager to secure one more lion or leopard skin for himself, to add new honors to his name, and new feathers to his cap.

This time the invader was a lion. With one bound, the startled beast leaped over the inclosure fence, carrying a half-grown ox in his mouth. But, seeing himself surrounded by enemies, he dropped the animal and bounded out of the compound between two huts, and away into the bush.

The men knew that unless he should make another catch that night he would surely return before morning to finish the ox, for he had scarcely begun to eat the prey. So all the small boys were sent back with orders to tie the dogs inside the huts.

After a somewhat lengthy conversation, the men decided to hide and await the lion's return. They chose their hiding places carefully, making sure that the breeze would not carry the man-scent in the direction from which

A lion expresses his feelings

the lion must enter the village. They crept into the shadows under *mealie* bins, behind brush heaps, or inside piles of grass bundles. There they waited and watched a long time. The moon rose higher and higher. The night was balmy and clear, just right for a lion hunt.

Would the lion return? Should they wait any longer? It was long after midnight. Suddenly there was a snapping of twigs, and the next moment the watchers saw the beast emerge from the circle of huts. He stepped out a few paces, and stood in the open compound, lashing his tail and looking from side to side. His heavy breathing could be heard distinctly. The magnificent animal crept stealthily up to the dead ox, smelled him over, and began to eat. He lay down by the carcass and ate rapidly, crunching the bones with evident delight. Now and then he would raise his head and look cautiously around, then continue eating. He ate as if this were his first meal for many days.

Not one of the men moved. After a time the lion seemed to become bolder, and to forget his fear. He was eating quite steadily now, without stopping to look around. The men still waited. They were used to the game. They would let him eat until he was too full and too clumsy to run well.

Nearly half of the ox was devoured. The lion now began to eat more slowly, going from side to side to pick out the most choice parts. Suddenly, without warning, Malambo gave a war whoop. He and his men jumped up and rushed forward. As they did so, each man threw his spear at the lion, and ran on past him. The bewildered beast was struck in several places. He rose to his full height, took a swift glance about him, then charged Malambo's brother. The man dodged to one side just in time and threw his spear, which struck the lion on the shoulder.

The creature was dazed, and could not decide which way to run, for all about him were men with pointed spears. The men came in closer and continued to throw their spears. One man would throw, then run on past the lion; another would follow him, doing the same. The lion saw that he was trapped. He gave a loud roar of pain and anger, and then turned to run. The men fell back a little. But he had eaten so much that he was heavy. Again they were upon him with their spears, and inflicted several severe wounds. By this time, he was fast losing strength.

When Malambo saw that the lion was too weak to do much harm, he came boldly forward and caught the great beast by his beautiful mane. Then all fear left the men. Some caught him by the tail, others laid their hands against his sides. All the men wished the honor of having handled aJiving lion. They would be considered men of renown, great hunters who were worthy of high respect.

The lion gave a final roar, and dropped dead.

8
A Quarrel

"Is it not time for you to go herding, my son?" Malambo asked of Choma one morning.

"I go with Kaluwe today, father," the boy replied. Choma picked up his long, rawhide whip, which was standing in the corner of the hut. He took his "piano" from a basket that hung on the wall. "I go," he said, stepping outside and giving a loud call: "Kaluwe! Kaluwe!"

A boy came running, whip in one hand and bow and arrow in the other. The two boys took a pot with some meal in it, and started out. When they reached the cattle kraal, they found the men still milking. Two picanins were stationed at the gate, admitting the calves one by one, as the milkers called for them.

As soon as a calf was let in, it ran straight to its mother and began to suck. When the milker thought the calf had drunk its share of milk, he pulled it off, and called one of the numerous picanins to guard it, while he tied the cow's legs with a leather thong, and took what milk was left for himself. Occasionally the little calf would squirm loose and get to its mother. Whenever this happened, a sharp rap on its nose reminded the little creature that it was out of order.

Milupi was milking seven cows that belonged to his father. He got about two or three cups of milk from each one. While milking, he squatted on the ground, on the left side of the cow, and milked with one hand at a time, while he held a small earthen bowl with the other. As each cow was milked, the bowl of milk was handed to one of the picanins, who carried it away to the hut.

A boy held the calf while the man finished milking

The boys must herd the cattle

Choma at Home

The calves were driven out into the fields by two herd boys, while Choma and Kaluwe drove the rest of the cattle away in another direction.

All day they must watch to see that none of them strayed off or were lost. The pasture was poor, for the old grass had nearly all been burnt, and the new grass was small and scattering. This made the cattle restless, and the boys had all they could do to watch them and keep them together.

In the afternoon the cattle became tired of roaming, and began to lie down and rest. The boys amused themselves setting snares for birds, and playing their "piano."

This was made of a set of metal keys arranged on a frame over the mouth of a small calabash. They held it between their hands and picked the strings with their fingers. It took the place for them of the mouth organ American children play.

They were growing very hungry, and had caught nothing in the snares, but they shot a pheasant with their bow and arrow. Finding a smoldering brush pile, they made a fire of sticks and roasted the bird. They also cooked the corn meal they had brought with them.

After eating their food, as the cattle were still resting, the two boys lay down under a tree for a sleep. But while they slept, their herd wandered off. When they awoke, no cattle could be seen. After much trouble, they found them, mixed with a herd from another village, and succeeded in separating their own from the others. But when they counted their cows, they discovered one was missing..They knew that it must be in the other herd, which was now being driven rapidly away from them. But the other herd boys refused to give it up.

Choma and Kaluwe pursued them, and claimed their cow. "Look!" they shouted. "Look at its ears! Four notches in one ear and two in the other! None of your cattle have that mark. Look at your cows! Three notches in one ear and none in the other!"

But the other boys insisted that their father had bought this cow from a man in Malambo's village after its ears had been snipped. Choma and Kaluwe started to drive the bewildered cow back to their own herd. But the boys objected, threatening them. Then they came to blows. They flew at one another. The fight was on. How they pounded, -with fists and then with sticks and stones! And the dust flew! Oh, how it flew!

Choma and Kaluwe were badly bruised. But they did not give up until they had secured their cow. To have gone home without it would have meant punishment and disgrace. Two battered and bruised little boys returned home that night; but they walked with the air of generals returning from the conquest of the world.

9
Planting Time

One morning before daylight, Ba-ka-Milupi got up and called the children. "Come," she said. "We must go to the fields and plant. Last night, when the sun went down, we saw in the east the sign that planting is here." It was the little group of stars that we call the "Pleiades."

Mother tied baby Luwo on her back. She put a few live coals into the firepot. Nzala and Choma picked up the short-handled, narrow-bladed, bluntedged hoes, and Malambo fastened a calabash of water on a spear over his shoulder. He was going with his people today to see that the lands were ready for the women and children to plant.

The children snatched up a few handfuls of peanuts to eat along the way. No one in an industrious African family thinks of stopping for breakfast during planting time.

Nearly all the people of the village tramped away to their cornfields that morning. Only the old people stayed at home to watch the fires and guard the huts.

When the family reached their garden plot, they cleared the ground of dry grass roots and old cornstalks, gathered them into heaps, and burned them. At noon, when the sun grew hot, they returned to the village to eat and rest. Grandma had cooked the food, and had set it in the sun to keep warm for them. When they returned she was sitting on the ground by the food dishes, guarding them from the village dogs.

In the afternoon, Malambo and some of the older men of the village carried baskets of *mealies* to the "prophet." The old man accepted the full baskets that they brought, and in return, gave them a few handfuls of *mealies* that he had blessed and mixed with medicine powder. As the people received them, they patted their hands together softly to show their thankfulness. They took the "medicine-*mealies*," home to mix with their own seed corn. They thought the "medicine-*mealies*" would help their seed to grow well and yield a good crop.

Every morning, before sunrise, Ba-ka-Milupi and her children returned to the fields to plant. Malambo usually remained in the village and attended to his duties as headman. Little Luwo laughed and cooed and cried and wriggled about on his mother's back, while she bent over and loosened little circles of the hard earth and dropped one or two corn kernels in each hill. When he went to sleep, he was laid on the ground in the shade of a tree, and covered with the baby-blanket.

Day after day the people went to their fields. In the middle of the day, when the sun was hot, they returned to their huts to rest, going back again to their fields late in the afternoon. When all the gardens were planted, they waited for the rain. There were a few light showers, just enough to sprout the grain. But the rains stopped coming, and the sprouted grain began to wilt.

The sun grew hotter and hotter. People looked at one another in dismay. "Unless we have a big rain," they said, "the sprouted grain will die in the ground and there will be a famine." Malambo and his men went again to see the "prophet," to inquire why the rain was delayed. "The spirit of your great chief is displeased with you," the old man answered, "You must make beer for him, and bring him gifts."

So the village women took their precious meal and began to make it into beer for the spirit of their dead chief.

10
Praying for Rain

Early one morning the people of the village gathered near Malambo's hut. The woman had brought pots of beer. They were going to their old chief's grave to ask his spirit to plead with *Leza* (God)* to send them rain.

The poor people needed their corn for food. Their grain bins were nearly empty. They would have many hungry days before green herbs grew again in the fields. But if they did not make beer in honor of their dead chief, his spirit would not help them get rain. *Leza* would forget them, no food would grow, and they would all starve. So they took their precious corn, ground it fine, cooked it, and left it to sour into beer.

Slowly the procession left the village and filed down the path. The men went ahead with their spears, to drive off any enemies or wild beasts that they might meet. Next came the herd boys driving a black ox for an offering. The women and children followed, carrying pots of beer on their heads. The dogs trotted along beside them.

The people walked and walked all the forenoon in the hot sun. On their way they passed the village where the priest lived, and he joined the procession. A little before noon, they came to the chief's grave. A small hut about four feet high had been erected near the chief's grave as a home for the great spirit. When the hut was built, a fence of green poles was made around it. These poles had sprouted and grown into a hedge of thick green.

Several small pots were standing by the hut. The people were very careful of them. The chief had promised that as long as the pots remained unbroken they might come to him when they needed rain, and he would help them.

Malambo gave the priest the offering that he and his people had brought, who presented it to the spirit in the hut. While he was doing this, the people looked on in silence. He also poured a little beer into each one of the pots. The hot sun would dry up the beer, and the people would say, "The spirit has come; he is pleased with us; he has drunk the beer that we gave him."

As the priest presented the offering he spoke to the spirit: "Hear us, O thou spirit of our great and mighty warrior! Look at the gift your poor people have brought you. Be not angry. Send *Leza* to help us, lest we die of hunger."

---

* These people call God *"Leza."* Some of them think of Him as the Creator, others merely as the rain itself, because the rain brings them life.

When the priest had finished speaking, Malambo gave him his present. It was a black fowl. One of the women brought the fire pot, and lighted a pile of dry grass and sticks. Others ran here and there for dry branches and piled the wood high on the fire. The ox was roasted, and there was a feast. The people ate the meat and drank beer. After this they danced and played.

Toward evening, when it began to get cool, the priest called the people together. He said to them, "Rain is coming! Run, or you will get wet. If *Leza* is pleased with your gifts, he will come and wash out your foot prints." The people returned to their villages.

But the rain did no come. The people complained to the priest. "You must come to the grave again," he said, "and you must bring me a better present. I wish two oxen."

"Aha!" the people said, "that is why there is no rain. The priest wanted a better present." So they brought his present, and also two black goats as an offering to the spirit, and went again to the grave for another feast and dance.

"Now *Leza* is pleased," the priest said, as he accepted the two oxen and gave them to his herd boy to drive away to his village. Then they prayed to the spirit again, and danced and feasted and drank beer.

Rain came at last, not because of the feasting and dancing, but because some rain is almost sure to fall every year in the rainy season. But it was so late that all the fields had to be planted again. The village people worked early and late, taking their food with them to the fields, so that they would not have to return to their huts at noon.

11
Seeking Food

The food supply in the village was about used up. The beer-making had emptied the grain bins. There were no green herbs yet in the fields. The cattle had not returned from the lowlands. While waiting for the rain to come, the women and children took their hoes and went into the fields to dig for roots that they could eat. Some took baskets and went to gather fruit that grew wild on thorny little trees.

Others went to the palm forest and gathered the nuts that lay thick on the ground. These palm nuts look like tiny cocoanuts. Their meat is not good to eat, for they are filled with "vegetable ivory," a substance as hard as bone. But their soft, fibrous husks taste sweet when chewed up. The women carried basketfuls of these nuts back to the village. They scraped off the soft, woolly husks, and packed them away in earthen jars for food.

One day the men and boys decided to go hunting. The people chopped up some medicine roots and put them in a *nonga* of water. Before daylight the next morning the hunters washed their spears in the medicine water. They also burned roots in the fire, and held their spears in the smoke. They thought the medicine would help their spears fly straight. While it was still dark, they glided silently and swiftly down the path to the river. The dogs trotted quietly at their heels.

Along the river banks, strips of grass had been left unburnt. The buck and other wild animals came to the river to drink from the water holes. At night

African women carry their jars of food or drink on their heads

these little creatures would feed, and in the morning they would lie down and sleep, hidden behind ant hills in the tall grass.

When the men reached the river, they selected a patch of thick grass and surrounded it. Quietly they closed in, making a circle. Then they began to shout. The little wild animals were startled. They sprang up and began to run. All about them they saw men with spears. First they ran in one direction, then in another, only to be driven back by the spears. Frightened and bewildered by the beating of drums, the blowing of horns, and the barking of dogs, they were easily killed.

The hunt continued all day. Many buck were killed, and there was food again in the village.

12
The Witch Doctor

"Baby Luwo is sick," said his mother. "He has taken little food for two days. He cries, and his head is hot. We must learn who is troubling us."

Malambo took a spear and went at once to the witch doctor. "I have trouble," he said.

The witch doctor accepted the present Malambo had brought. Then he offered his visitor a stool and, seating himself on the ground, said, "Your wife is ill at home."

"Yes, that is it," Malambo replied. The witch doctor knew then that he had made a mistake. The father must lie to the witch doctor, so as to test him and see if he can discover the truth for himself.

The witch doctor guessed again. "Your cattle have strayed away, and are lost," he ventured this time.

"Yes, that is it," replied Malambo, and the doctor knew that he had missed it again.

The witch doctor guessed again and again. Every time that Malambo said, "Yes," he knew that he had made a mistake.

At last he said, "Your baby is ill."

"No! no!" said Malambo, "my baby is well, very well." The witch doctor knew then that he had guessed right.

"Yes, that is it, your, baby is ill; you have been lying to me," he repeated. Malambo assented. "The witch doctor is very clever," thought Malambo, as he watched the old man take from his belt a small skin bag with four bones in it. These had been carved from the back bone of an elephant. The witch doctor shook the bones well, and threw them out on the floor of the hut. He looked carefully at them, then picked them up one at a time and smelled of each one.

"It is not a living person that is bewitching your child," he said.

He put the bones back in the bag, rattled them again, threw them on the floor, then picked them up and smelled of each one. "It is the spirit of one of your people, and not of your wife's people, who is troubling the child," he said.

Again he shook and threw the bones, and sat studying them a long time. He picked out one bone and smelled of it several times. "The spirit of your father's sister is displeased with you because you never speak of her, and because her beer pot is always empty."

"Aha!" said Malambo. "We have little beer for ourselves these days of hunger."

He went home at once, and told his wife to bring beer. She poured it into a bowl, and placed the bowl by the door way. Then they both spoke to the spirit. "Look!" they said. "See the present we have brought you. Come and drink, and be displeased no more. Pity us in our trouble, and take away the sickness from our child."

She poured the rest of the beer on the ground for any other spirits that might be feeling neglected at the time.

But Baby Luwo continued to grow worse. He no longer laughed and cooed, but lay quite still. Once in awhile he would cry out as if in pain. And he would drink no milk.

Again Malambo went to the witch doctor, and watched him shake the magic bones. He announced that the spirit of the great-aunt was appeased but added," There are many spiteful spirits of enemies that are troubling your child now. I will send you to a medicine man who will give you powerful medicine to drive the evil spirits away.

13
The Medicine Doctor

Malambo at once sought the medicine doctor. He gave him some leaves, root, and bark of a medicine tree, and told him how to use it. For this favor, Malambo promised to send him a hoe.

When the father reached his home, he took some glowing embers from the fire and placed them on a piece of broken dish. Then he laid some of the medicine on the embers, and it began to smoke. Ba-ka-Milupi gave the baby some tea made from the medicine leaves. Then she held him close to the smoking medicine. Baby did not like the smell, and turned his face away. She held him closer to it. His nose was smarting, and tears were rolling from his poor little eyes. He choked and spluttered. Then he screamed out with all the strength he had.

"Aha!" cried Malambo, "Look! Look! The evil spirit has left the child. There he goes! Now our baby will get well."

Baby Luwo was covered with sweat. He was too tired and weak to cry any longer, and fell asleep in his mother's arms. When he awoke, he drank a little milk.

No evil spirits had been troubling him. The little pieces of corn-meal porridge that had been given to him from time to time had made him ill. The porridge was too coarse, and had not been cooked long enough. The medicine tea cleansed and soothed his poor, sore little stomach; and as he had refused all food for several days, his stomach had rested long enough to get well.

The people of the village said, "What a good medicine doctor we have! He has saved the baby's life."

The Dance

14
Getting Ready

There was to be a big dance in the village, and every body was busy getting ready for it. The women were scraping the grain bins clean for a last bit of grain that could be pounded into meal and used for making beer. Little girls were skipping about with babies on their backs almost as big as themselves. Boys were gathering palm roots, and preparing them for skirt-making. The men were sitting around, smoking, and bossing the workers.

To make the skirts the boys pounded the fibers of the palm roots between flat stones. The stringy mass was then washed in a water hole. Last of all, the big girls chewed it until the fibers were soft and white. Then they twisted and rolled them into string for fringe skirts.

Ba-ka-Milupi wished her little daughter to look well for the dance. She took a piece of red stone from one of the baskets hanging on the wall, dipped it in water, and rubbed it on a rock, until a thick, red paste was made. She mixed butter with the paste, and then rubbed it over her little girl's body. The polishing finished, Nzala looked like a piece of new furniture just from the shop.

The mother also rubbed some of the red paste over Nzala's black, wooly hair. Before it was dry, she wet her hand and rubbed it in the ash pile at the hut door. She added the mixture of ashes and dust to the greasy red paste on Nzala's head. When she had worked this thoroughly and evenly into the hair, she twisted it up into dozens of little curls that stuck out like corkscrews.

The little girl strung brightly colored beads on fiber thread, and her mother looped them into her curls. She tied a big white shell around her neck, and added a few strings of beads. Nzala put on her new fringe skirt of palm-root fiber, and slipped some extra ivory bangles on her arms, and some brass leglets on her legs.

"Our daughter is fair to look upon," said her mother.

"We shall get many cattle for her when she is married," her father added, with a satisfied air. Nzala knew that she was pretty. She bobbed her head about, making the beads clink. And she laughed and giggled, just as many small girls do in other countries.

Then the rest of the family polished up. Mother put on her beautiful leopard-skin skirt, her shells and beads, and extra bangles. She took off her old leather headband, and replaced it with one of beads. And although it was a very hot day, father put on his heavy brown overcoat. He had bought this from an English trader for two oxen and a cow. It seemed the most appropriate thing that he had for the grand occasion, because it was a part of the white man's wardrobe. He fastened a large white shell on his forehead, and tied several others around his arms and neck. Then he donned his gourd-shell cap trimmed with tufts of red feathers. Only brave warriors were permitted to wear this particular kind of red feather. Each feather stood for a lion, a leopard, or a man, that he had killed.

There was a little red paste left. Choma rubbed it on his legs and arms. He did admire shiny legs. He made a skull cap out of the bottom of a calabash, and fastened a large tuft of cock feathers in it. Then he tied on his shells, and polished his spears. He, too, was ready for the dance.

15
The Greetings

Early in the morning visitors began to arrive from the other villages. Lwimbo, the headman from the nearest village, came first with his people.

Malambo and his men had killed ten oxen for the feast. The boys were cutting up the meat, and the women were cooking it in large earthen pots over the open fire. When Lwimbo and his people arrived, Malambo, surrounded by the men of his village, was sitting in front of his hut, directing the work.

Malambo offered stools to Lwimbo and his men. As he did so, he greeted them. "You are seen," he said.

"Yes, we are seen. You also are seen," Lwimbo replied, as they all sat down.

Malambo called to a little girl who was passing:

"Bring the fire pot, so that my guests may light their pipes." As the men sat and smoked, they continued their greetings.

"Have you risen well?" Malambo asked Lwimbo.

"Yes, I have risen well. Have you also risen well?" he replied.

Malambo: "Yes, I have risen well. Are you alive?"

Lwimbo: "Yes, I am alive. Are you also alive?"

Malambo: "Yes, I am alive. Is your wife here?"

Lwimbo: "Yes, she is here. Is your wife here?"

Malambo: "Yes, she is here."

Lwimbo: "And the babe is well?"

Malambo: "Yes, it is well."

Lwimbo: "What are you and your people talking about?"

Malambo: "There is nothing to talk about. All is quiet. How is it where you come from?"

Lwimbo: "There also it is quiet."

When Malambo had finished the greetings with Lwimbo, he turned to another visitor, and repeated them all with him. He went through the entire list of questions with each one in turn.

At last the greetings were finished. The men continued to smoke and talk. More visitors were constantly arriving, and all the greetings had to be repeated. Thus they spent a long time in greetings. This story should help you to understand what Jesus meant when He sent out His disciples and told them to "greet no man by the way." He did not mean they should not speak to people, but that they should not waste time in long greetings that did not mean much.

The food for the feast was cooked in big jars over open fires

The women and children collected in little groups under the broad eaves of the huts. They also talked, and many of the women smoked. Now and then one of the village women would step out and stir the boiling meat, or add a little water.

A big waterpot of beer was brought out and set on the ground for the men. Each man produced a cup, or bowl, which he had brought with him from home. A young man sat by the pots, and dipped the beer out with a gourd-shell cup. The *indunas* (headmen) and other important men were served first, then the common folks, and last of all the boys. Other *nongas* of beer were brought out for the women and children, and. they also began to drink.

16
The Dance

All through the hot day the people smoked, and talked, and drank beer. New people kept coming and coming, until the whole village looked like a hive of swarming bees.

In the afternoon word was passed around that the meat was ready. The people sat down in groups of seven or eight. Young men were appointed to serve the meat. They were very carefully chosen for this honorable task. They must be trusty, so as to divide the meat fairly, and they must be strong so as to settle any quarrels that might arise over the food.

The meat was divided and put in earthen bowls. When it was all ready to serve, village boys carried a dish to each group of people.

After the feast was over, the village drums were brought out. The drummer boys used their hands for drumsticks. When one boy's hand became sore from pounding, another drummer boy would be chosen.

The boys and young men were gathered in a semicircle around one of the drummer boys. Two by two they came out and danced. The old men sat and talked.

The women gathered in another semicircle and danced, clapping their hands to keep time. Old, wrinkled grandmothers, little girls, and women with babies on their backs took turns in the dance.

They kept on dancing and drinking beer all the evening. When one of them became too drunk to stand up, he would wrap himself in his blanket and lie down by the fire to sleep. The dancing continued till nearly morning.

All the people from one village danced in a group by themselves, and those from the other villages did the same. Each group tried to dance the longest without stopping. The rivalry of the various groups sometimes led to disputes and fighting.

In the morning the village was a sad sight. Men and women were lying around on the ground among meat bones and broken beer cups. For three days the feasting and dancing continued. The last night was the worst of all. Men fought, children screamed, and everybody felt ill.

Nzala's mother called her family into the hut. "Children," she said, "sit here and care for grandma and baby. I must go and see that food and beer are offered to all the guests. These dances are very bad, very bad. I love them not."

The children obeyed, as all African children are taught to do, and gathered around the fire-stones in the hut. There they sat with grandma in the

The drummers for the dance used their hands for drumsticks

Photo by: E. Hughes, Luena, N. Rhodesia

center of the group, watching the fires in the compound, and listening to the drumming and clapping and shouting and dancing. They could see one another's faces quite clearly by the moonlight that shone through the open door, and through the little square window-hole.

And then, like all other boys and girls in all other lands, the children asked, "Give us a story, grandma. We want a story. Tell us about what you did when you were a little girl."

17
The Slave Raid

This is the story that grandma told the children. "When I was a little girl, I lived in a country many days' journey away. Our village was by a river that had water in it all the year, and yet whose banks were so high that it never overflowed the land. We planted gardens the entire year. The beans and peanuts that we grew were very good; the squashes were sweet, and their leaves made good relish. Our *mealie* fields were large. Many reed-buck and other wild animals came to the river to drink, and our men and boys speared them easily. We never knew hunger. My sister, Numba, and I had to gather wood and carry water and hoe the garden.

"But there were days when we could go with our two brothers and the other children of the village to play in the forest. There we would build play-huts. The girls would bring yams and *mealie* ears, and we would cook and eat. We chose some of the boys to be headmen; and we traded clay oxen, fought mimic battles, and captured slaves. We had little fear of lions, for we kept our fires burning; and as the wild game was so easy for them to get, they did not trouble in the day time. But the crocodiles were sly. We always threw rocks into the river, before going near enough to draw water. If any crocodiles lifted their heads out of the water to see what was making the disturbance, we took the warning, and ran away in terror. We had much happiness when we were children.

"But one terrible day the slave-catchers came to our village. My father had called my brothers early that morning. 'Come!' he said, 'we will begin today to make our new hut. Let us work before the sun is hot.' He loosened the bamboo door at the entrance to the hut and set it to one side. The boys were closely following him as he stepped outside, when suddenly two dark figures rushed out from behind a pile of poles.

"Father turned toward the hut, calling for mother to bring his spear. But it was too late; the men were upon him. He cried out to us, 'Run! Save yourselves!' Seeing that he could not help himself or the boys, he told my brothers to give themselves up quietly to the warriors and go with them. For he knew that if he or the boys tried to fight, the men would kill them, and then capture us. But while they were binding the men and leading them away to the guards waiting outside the stockade, there might be a chance for us to escape. He and the boys would watch their chance to get away and return to us.

"Mother sprang from her bed and caught up an ax. She whispered to us, 'Out of the window and run for the new grass pile!' In another instant Numba

The girls tried to hide among bundles of grass like these,
which are being used to roof the hut in the middle

and I were being shoved through the window-hole in the wall of our hut. It was still dusk. We crept cautiously along in the shadow of our *mealie* bins. The bundles of grass that we had gathered for our new hut were piled up against one of the bins. Mother shoved us toward this.

"She began to move one of the bundles, so as to hide us behind it. But just as she was doing this, we heard voices of men near by. Trembling with fear, we crouched in the shadow of the grass pile, and waited for them to pass. Then mother thought of an old ant-bear hole in the path, a few feet from where we were, that would make a safer hiding place for sister and me. She waited until no one was near, then picked up a stick and jabbed it vigorously into the hole to see if there were any animal inside. The hole seemed to be empty. She drew me toward it, and helped me to climb in. I clung to her hands as I slipped down, down, into the cold, dark hole. Every minute I expected to be bitten by some frightful creature.

"'Is there room there for Numba too?' mother whispered down to me. 'Yes,' I gasped, thankful at the thought of having company. Sister crawled into the hole with me. 'Be very quiet, and wait till I come for you,' and mother was gone.

18
Hiding

"There we stayed and waited, wedged in so tightly that we could scarcely move, and so terrified that our own breathing frightened us. Now and then we could hear men shouting and children screaming. Dogs were howling and cattle bawling. Once we heard the footsteps of people on the path overhead. The walls of our prison were damp, and at first we shivered with cold. But after a time it grew warmer.

"We dared not even look out of the hole. How we did long to see some one that we knew or to hear a familiar voice! We grew hungry. What had happened to father and the boys? Would mother never come to us? Had she been captured too? We cried, but very softly because we dared not make a noise. And we prayed to the spirit of our grandmother, as we always did when in trouble, and to all the other helpful spirits we could think of. We begged them to help us, and to save father and the boys, and to make mother invisible so the raiders could not see her.

"We knew that the medicine horn that mother usually wore around her neck, and without which she seldom ventured from the hut, was probably still hanging over the bed where she had put it the night before. If she had only taken this powerful charm with her, we should have been more hopeful. Father had purchased the horn from a powerful medicine man, and had given seven oxen for it. If there had only been time for mother to have put on the medicine horn before she fled that morning, we felt sure her chances for escape would have been better. None of her enemies could have seen her while she wore that powerful charm.

"There was one thought that gave us hope. Mother had been eating quail the day before. That would help her to hide quickly out of sight of the warriors.

"After what seemed to us days, I lifted Numba up so she could peek out of the hole. Not a person was in sight. The whole village was as still as night, although the sun was shining brightly overhead. 'Mother! mother!' we called softly. There was no answer. Oh, where was mother? Had everybody been carried away? Had we two little girls been left alone in the village to die? We were not very old. Sister was just getting her second teeth. I was a little older.

"We cried again, and then we slept—how long I do not know.

"When I awoke, mother's hand was on my head. We reached up and caught hold of it, and she pulled us out of the hole. It was past noon. We had been in the ant-bear hole more than half a day.

19
After the Raid

"The raiders had marched away, and it seemed as if they had taken the whole village with them. Not a living person was in sight. There were no cattle lowing now, for they had all been driven away. The air was full of smoke. Many of the huts, where our poor people had been peacefully sleeping a few hours before, were now only smoldering ash-heaps. Three hungry dogs came timidly up to us wagging their tails. How glad we were to see even them!

"Our own hut was still standing. Cautiously we crept inside and looked about. But we were afraid to stay here long, so we crawled into one of the grain bins, and sat down on the floor. We were hidden from the window-hole by a heap of unshelled kafir corn. Numba and I laid our heads on mother's knees, and then we all three cried together. We remained hidden there all the rest of the day until the sun went down and it began to grow dark.

"Mother told us that while we children were in the ant-bear hole she had been hiding in the pile of grass bundles. She had been able to see much that was going on about her. Two of the village boys had been led by the raiders down the path near our hiding place. Their hands were fastened behind them, and they had ropes around their waists. It must have been their footsteps that we heard while we were in the ant-bear hole.

"It was supposed that the warriors had come during the night, as the slave raiders usually did, had climbed the stockade of poles that surrounded the village, and had distributed themselves, two or three men at each hut. When our people had opened their doors in the morning, the men had sprung upon them, tied their hands, and led them away.

"Before the sun was like this [grandma pointed to a point in the sky midway between the eastern sky and overhead] mother heard the company of people tramping away. Her husband, her sons, some of her brothers and sisters, and many of her neighbors were being marched away to be sold as slaves in a strange country. Finally the noise died down, the bawling of the cattle became fainter and fainter, then all was quiet. Mother had waited a long time after this before she dared to pull us out of the hole.

"At night we went back to our hut again. One by one those who had escaped crept out of their hiding places. Few people had been killed, but many had been captured. Only those who tried to defend themselves were injured. Some had successfully fought their way through the circle of warriors stationed around the village. They had hidden in *mealie* fields, or behind ant-hills in the tall grass.

"The day after the raid, our little band of survivors followed for a short way the footprints leading out of the village, then we turned back in despair to our lonely homes. We had no weapons, and there were too few of us to attempt a rescue.

"We gathered together some food and blankets, and fled to the forest, leaving the village entirely deserted for many days. From time to time, our men would steal cautiously back to the village in the night to get fresh supplies of food. We did not return until we learned that the raiding army had left the country.

"Only once did we hear any news of our people who had been captured. One of the men managed to escape and get back to our village, He told us that some of the captives were taken by the raiders to become slaves in their own villages. But the stronger ones, including our father and brothers, were sold to Arab slavers. As they marched along, they were joined by other companies of slaves who had been captured in other villages, and they were all driven in one company toward the great waters far to the east. The men had their necks fastened in heavy forked sticks. The women were roped waist to waist. All were given loads of rubber or ivory to carry on their heads. The children were left free to run along by their mothers' sides. One old man died by the way. A young mother became too weak to nurse her baby. When the little one cried, the slavers knocked it in the head, and left it to die beside the road.

"For years we had hopes that our dear ones would come back to us, but they never returned. One day had changed our happy and prosperous village into a lonely and desolate place. There were many, many villages that suffered in the same way. Of some families only one or two persons remained. We cared for the orphan children, and comforted the lonely as best we could. But every heart was broken.

"My mother's sister had been hurried away without having time to go back for her sleeping babe. We took the little one. He became our brother, and helped us to forget our sorrows.

20
The Unlucky Baby

"We suffered greatly that first year after the raid. We had no milk, for our cattle were all gone. Much of our other property had been taken also. We had so few spears that hunting was difficult. Only a few hoes could be found in the village with which to dig our gardens.

"I wished for the time to come when I should be married, for I knew that then mother would get hoes, and cattle, and such other things as she might wish to ask for me. I was married while still very young. I could work well, and was fair to look upon. My husband was kind to me. He seldom beat me.

"When my baby was born, I was once more happy. For a time I forgot all the trouble of the past. At night my husband would often come into the hut and sit with me by the fire. While he told stories, I would take our baby on my knee and play with him. How the child would laugh whenever his father poked the fire to make the sparks fly. He liked the child, and would often say, 'Our son will be a headman some day. Aha! He is a wise child. He will become a great chief.'

"One day I noticed a small, white spot on the baby's upper gum. Could it be a tooth that was coming *there?* I felt of his gum with my finger. It was true. His upper teeth were coming first. Our baby was an unlucky child. My heart was filled with fear. I determined to hide the fact from my people, and risk the displeasure of all the family ghosts, rather than to part with my baby.

When anything is going on in a village, like a dance,
the women and children gather around like this

"Oh, how eagerly I looked for the lower teeth! But they were slow in coming. One day my mother noticed me examining the baby's mouth, and she discovered what had happened. 'The teeth have come in the wrong way,' she said; 'you cannot keep your child, for he would grow up to be as dangerous as a mad dog. If he should bite some one, and that person should die, the people of our village would take revenge and kill all our family.'

"Then, seeing my grief, she aid to me, 'Do not cry. If you do, your next child also will be unlucky.' Mother and Numba and I formed a little procession; and early in the morning, we went down to the river. They tried to comfort me. 'Poor little baby,' they said, 'it is a pity you came, but you must go home, much as we should like to keep you. Good-bye, little one! Go away!' Then we dropped it into the river for a crocodile to pick up.

21
Mianda

"By and by we had a baby boy, and after that two girls. They were all lucky children; their lower teeth came in first. I was happy for many years. But again trouble followed me.

"There was a young man in a near-by village who wanted to marry Mianda, our oldest girl. She loved him, but his father was poor. Sickness had killed his oxen. He could not help his son to get the *lobola* (the gift to the bride's father). We were willing to wait until he could get the oxen. So the young people planned to be married.

"One night a stranger who was traveling through the country stayed over night at our village. When he saw Mianda he offered us many cattle for her. He had a wife and children already, but he was rich. We were poor. There was a famine in the country. We had little to eat. My husband said, 'We must take the cattle. If we do not, we may all die of hunger.'

"So my little girl went to live with this man, to be his wife. I shall never forget how she pleaded with us not to send her away. My heart was broken for my poor little girl. We all worked very hard, hoping that some time we could buy her back and bring her home. The young man who wanted to marry her told me secretly that he intended to have her husband killed by witchcraft. But I pleaded with him not to do so, as that would surely bring trouble on us all.

"Once Mianda came home to us. She had run away from her new home. She was thin and looked old. Her hands were hard from hoeing, and her back and legs were scarred from beatings. She begged us to return the *lobola,* and to let her stay with us. But we had nothing to pay.

"The man came after her. She tried to hide; but he found her, and took her back with him. Before the next planting time she was dead.

"Not long after this my son, my only boy, became sick and died. The other little girl grew to be a woman. She is your mother. Now you and your mother are all that I have left on earth. Trouble has always followed me."

Grandma paused, and dropped her head in her hands. Choma laid a loving hand on her shoulder. "I wonder," he asked, "if we shall all have as much trouble as you have had."

"Everybody has trouble, People are born for it," answered grandma.

The children sat quietly, not knowing what to say. They had been so happy, and had known so little of trouble yet, that they could not understand. They had heard grandma's stories many times; and they knew that there was one more yet to come.

22
Accused and Killed

"My husband and I took Nomai, our one little girl, and left the village where we had suffered so much. After consulting the witch doctor, we decided to go to a certain village where he said we should find good luck. We packed some of our household goods in baskets, which Nomai and I could carry on our heads, and some we tied in bundles that we could carry on our backs. My husband carried food. He also drove the cattle. After traveling all day, we reached the new village. There we built a hut and planted garden.

"Most of the people there were good to us. But one man quarreled with my husband. One of the first things we had done when we reached the new village was to choose a garden spot, and tie knots in the tall grass to show that we wished to plant there. But this man wanted the land that we had chosen. He became angry, and said that before we took possession of the land, we should have asked permission of the headman of the village. My husband confessed that he was in the wrong. He gave up the land, and chose another field.

"During the winter this man became sick and died. The people in the village thought that some one had bewitched him. The father and brothers and cousins of the dead man called the witch doctor to help them find out who had caused his death.

"The relatives were together with the witch doctor in their hut for a long time, while he consulted his bones. My husband was not much alarmed. He trusted the words of the witch doctor back in the old village who had promised him good luck. When the men came out of the hut, all the people in the village were frightened, though they tried not to show it.

"The men walked straight to our hut, and surrounded my husband. My heart was sick. They had decided that he had taken revenge on the man for quarreling with him, and had cast an evil eye upon him and killed him. They took my husband, who had never hurt anybody they took him out that night and speared him to death.

"After he was dead, I went out and stood by a pool of water. I intended to throw myself in. But who would care for Nomai? It would be cruel to leave her alone with out friends in a strange village. I decided to live for my child, and went back to our lonely little home.

"Trouble has always followed me. Now I am old. Soon I shall go—I know not where. Will trouble follow me there? Shall I ever see my dear ones who have been taken away from me?"

Then Grandma told the children a new story that they had never heard before.

23
The Legend*

"Once there was an old woman who wished to ask *Leza* [God] why she had so much trouble. She said, 'God has beset me before and behind. He has laid His hand upon me, and has taken away all that I ever loved, all that ever loved me, even to my children's children.'

"The old woman decided to find God, and ask Him why. Somewhere up there in the sky must be God's dwelling. If only she could reach it! She began to build a tower to reach to heaven. But again and again it fell.

"She could not reach God in that way. But somewhere there must be a road to Him. Far in the distance there was a place where the sky seemed to touch the earth. Surely if she could get there, she could find God.

"So she set out on her long journey, saying over and over to herself: 'I shall come to where the earth ends, and there where earth and sky touch I shall find a road to God, and I shall ask Him: "Why have you sent me so much trouble? Why have you taken away from me all that I ever loved, all that ever loved me?"'

"As she went through many lands, the people asked her: 'What have you come for, old woman? Where are you going all alone?'

"And she replied, 'I am seeking God.'

"'Seeking God? What for?'

"'He has taken away from me all that I ever loved, all that ever loved me. I am left alone in the world. I want to ask Him why.'

"They said, 'No one has ever found God. You are no different from others. God sends trouble to us all.'"

The story was finished. Nzala looked up into grandma's face. "Did the old woman ever find God?" she asked.

Grandma placed a shaking hand on the little girl's head as she answered: "The old woman never found God; no one has ever found Him; and from that day to this, her question has never been answered."

---

* Adapted from "The Ila-Speaking People of Northern Rhodesia," by E.W. Smith and A. Dale Murray.

The Missionary's Visit
24
Oleta at Home

"Mama, I'm tangled." Mother loosened the mosquito netting cage around her little girl's bed. Oleta hopped out.

Wallie and Toots had promised to play on the grass pile. Oleta must be up early, because after breakfast it would be too hot to play outside. The mission boys had been combing grass for thatching the new workshop. In the yard back of Oleta's house they had left a big pile of grass that was too short to use. The soft, fluffy grass pile was a delightful place in which to romp with the dogs.

There were three houses at the mission station. The mission director and his wife lived in one house. Wallie and Toots and their baby brother lived in another. Their father was the farm manager. Oleta lived in: the other house. Her father was the mission school teacher.

Every morning at six o'clock, when the big bell rang for the mission boys to go to work, he would go down to the school house and give lessons to the native teachers. He taught them Bible, and physiology, and history, and reading, and arithmetic; and he showed them how to teach these things to the boys and girls in the school.

At quarter to nine, when the dispensary bell rang, Oleta liked to run over and see if there were any sick babies to be treated. Very often there were little burned babies, When the babies in the villages begin to crawl and walk about, they sometimes fall into the open fire in the huts. Little babies with bad sores from neglected burns are brought in twenty and thirty miles to the mission.

The director's wife looked after the babies herself, while a native boy in white cap and apron bathed and bandaged sore legs and arms. After the babies were cared for, she would give medicine to the others.

The dispensary itself wasn't much to see. It was a little whitewashed brick building, about as big as an ordinary kitchen, and so old that the walls were about ready to fall out. But they had been fastened together at the top with strong wires that were stretched from side to side like clothes lines.

The cupboards for medicines were made of kerosene boxes, set on tin cans, to keep out the white ants. Kerosene tins served as foot tubs, and cooking oil tins for buckets, and condensed milk tins for cups. Sometimes the

The Missionary's Visit 51

medicines ran so low that a boy had to be sent around to the mission homes to borrow. And once in a while when the bandages gave out the missionary lady had to tear up her good aprons or her husband's shirts to use in dressing wounds.

Nine o'clock was breakfast time at Oleta's house. Daddy came in from the school, and Oleta from play, and mother from the hut, which served as an office, where she had been copying lessons on the typewriter.

Two African boys are teaching Oleta and her playmates to make clay oxen, while her mother is copying lessons in the office

Worship came directly after breakfast, and Oleta prayed for big brother and big sister, who were far away, and for all the people on the mission. After breakfast, daddy answered questions for the boys that came to the house. While this was going on, Oleta did her lessons. She sang from the "Sunshine Song Book" that the children in the homeland love so well, and learned her Bible story. Next she read about Peter and Joan, and printed the new words in her exercise book.

Then came sewing. Oleta was a busy mother. She had four children, not counting Teddy, to sew for. Teddy didn't need clothes, because, you see, he was a bear.

Nearly every day, when it came time for mother to set dinner cooking, Oleta went to the kitchen and helped, because the kitchen boy was in school at this time. After her part of the work was finished, she usually sat on the kitchen table or on a high stool, where she could see and ask questions about everything that was being done.

While the dinner was cooking, she went with mother to the schoolhouse to help daddy teach. She passed the pencils and chalk, and rang the bell. When there was nothing else to do, she drew pictures on the blackboard until mother's classes were finished.

The mission director's wife was the nicest lady for a little girl of four to visit. She had a woolly white dog, and a mother cat with six kittens that had each a different kind of face. And there were two little monkeys that chattered and squealed, and that would come up and take carrots and turnips out of her hand.

After dinner, everybody lay down to rest for half an hour. Oleta usually slept with both eyes and both ears open. The minute the clock struck four, she was up and away. By this time it was cool enough to play out side again.

Late in the afternoon, daddy would put Oleta on his bicycle and they would ride down to the garden together. She had her own little vegetable garden to care for, with one row each of carrots, and onions, and beets, and peas, and beans.

In the evening came the story hour, and prayers, and bedtime, and pleasant dreams till morning. And so the days passed by, week after week and month after month, until vacation time came.

25
Getting Ready for a Trip

School was closed for a month. The mission boys would be busy all day now, fertilizing, and plowing, and getting ready to plant as soon as the first heavy rains should come.

During school days, the boys spent half their time in school, and the other half working on the farm to pay for their food and schooling. In vacation time they worked all day to earn their shirts and trousers.

Later on, when the rains were over, and the corn was ready for harvesting, there would be another vacation in which the boys could earn their blankets.

So twice a year, when school was out, daddy went on visiting tours among the villages. This time mother and Oleta were going along for company. This was to be both an out-school trip and a preaching tour. They were going to visit some Christian villages where mission boys were teaching, and some heathen villages also, where no missionary had ever preached a sermon.

What a busy time it was getting ready for the trip! They were going to be a long way from any grocery stores, and must take all their provisions with them. Oleta helped mother bake oatmeal crisps, and cocoanut cookies, and date rolls, and pack them in oatmeal tins. She carried rice and sugar and flour and salt and other things from the pantry to the kitchen for Samuel, the kitchen boy, to put in the food box with the pots and dishes needed on the trip.

That night Oleta took Teddy and Baby Rose to bed with her, to be sure not to forget them in the morning, for they were to go with her on the trip.

Betsy Bobbit could not go. She was a birthday present from grandpa's friends away over in America; and mother thought Beautiful Betsy had better not risk the dangers of the trip.

When Oleta woke up in the morning, daddy was bending over her little bed, saying something like this: "I guess Oleta is too sleepy to go with us; we'd better leave her at home to take care of kitty." Of course Oleta jumped out of bed at once. It was still dark, but lanterns were burning. She had her cold bath, and was dressed in a wink. Her mama pinned her spine protector* inside her dress, and Oleta put on her cork helmet.

She looked out through the veranda screen. The mission wagon, drawn by eight oxen, was already at the door. Daddy was tying up bedding rolls. He

---

* The spine protector is a strip of khaki cloth lined with red, that is worn in the tropics to protect the nerves in the backbone from the direct rays of the sun.

lifted the food box into the front of the wagon for a seat, and covered it with blankets. Then Paul, the house boy, piled on the bedding rolls, the suit case, and the little phonograph. Samuel brought a kerosene tin full of boiled water for drinking, and hung the canvas water-bag by its hook to one of the four poles that supported the awning.

Peter; one of the native teachers in the mission school, was going along as interpreter. He had been at the mission for many years, and spoke good English. Samuel was going to do the cooking. Besides these, there were a driver and two leader boys. They all had blanket rolls, which were piled on the wagon at the back; and they also brought a bag of corn meal, two pots, and a calabash of salt. A big piece of canvas was spread carefully over the things in the wagon. There was likely to be rain before the party would have returned to the mission station.

At last everything and everybody were ready—except—oh, of course there were the usual trips to the house for the alarm clock, the hymn books, and something else that had almost been forgotten! Then, *"Hamba* [go]!" shouted the driver, as he vigorously cracked his whip. One of the leader boys grasped the cowhide reins that were attached to the horns of the front oxen. They began to move, and the old wagon rolled slowly out of the mission compound and across the fields. Peter rode his bicycle on ahead, so he could reach the village before the party arrived and give them a greeting from the mission. Samuel and the other leader boy walked along behind the wagon. When the first leader boy got tired, the second one would take a turn.

Oleta liked to play she was an African woman

26
The Journey

The oxen were lazy old fellows, quite determined to walk all the way. Once in a while, by means of much shouting and cracking of the whip, they were made to trot for a time. But usually, just as they got into an easy trot, the wagon wheels would go chug, chug into an ant-bear hole, or would hit a stump. Boxes and bundles would tumble about in the wagon, and everybody would bounce. Oleta's helmet would fall off, and daddy would put one arm around his little girl and grasp the awning pole with the other, allowing his notebook and Chitonga grammar and pencils to scatter to the floor. Then the oxen would drop again into a walk.

One extra big jolt sent the canvas water-bag flying from its nail overhead. Before it could be righted, Mother's dress was so wet that she decided to get out and walk. Without stopping the wagon, she slipped off at the back. Daddy jumped over the wheel, and then helped Oleta out. The oxen crawled along, switching their tails at the flies, and trying to snatch a tuft of grass, much to the annoyance of the leader boy, who jerked them vigorously back with the leather thong.

Oleta was happy now, for with daddy's help she could reach the flowers that grew on the trees by the roadside. But she had to be careful in picking them, for nearly every tree was bristling with long, spiny thorns. The whole family enjoyed the early morning walk so well that it became the regular program on out-school trips.

By the time they had reached the river, where it was planned to stop to water the oxen and eat breakfast, it was eleven o'clock. The wagon had traveled about fourteen miles in five hours. Everyone in the party, especially the driver, was glad to stop and rest.

The leader boys quickly outspanned the oxen and led them to water. One of the boys watched them while they grazed. The other boy gathered firewood and made a fire. He brought water from the river, and cooked *mealie* porridge, and made peanut butter sauce for the native workers.

Samuel soon had his fire going and was cooking breakfast for the missionaries.

"Um! Um! How good those fried eggs smell, mama, and the postum, and even the oatmeal porridge! I'm so hungry, I don't see how I can wait another minute."

"Maybe you would like to hurry the breakfast along by helping me set the table. Put those date rolls on that aluminum plate, and set them right in the middle of the table," mother directed.

Oleta picked up one of the date rolls. "Oh, mummie, can't I have one now? I'm so hungry!"

"Isn't it delightful to be hungry when there's so much good food waiting to be eaten? Now run and call daddy." He was having a chat with an English trader who happened to be camping near by.

After breakfast the dishes were cleared away and taken down to the river to be washed. Then the hymn books were brought out, and everybody sang, "Shall we gather at the river?" "Toiling for Jesus," and others of the good old songs that people love the world around. The words were different from those that we sing in the homeland; but they had the same meaning and could be sung to the same tunes.

After the singing, Daddy read some of God's precious promises, and they prayed that God would help them to find in the Bible just the message that the people in the villages most needed to hear, and that He would make them willing to listen to it.

It was a happy hour. Both Peter and Samuel had once joined in wild, drunken dances with the other people in their home villages. It had been only a few months since the other boys had been leading that kind of life. Now they were all singing songs to the praise of Jesus. Somewhere over there in those thatched villages to which the mission party were going were others who would gladly listen to the words of life and who, in their turn, would carry the good news to their brothers who were waiting for the light.

After worship everybody rested under the trees—everybody except Oleta. Time was too precious for her to sleep. And there were so many interesting things to see, and so many beautiful leaves from which to make wreaths. In the evening while the oxen jogged along, and the big people were watching for bright eyes that might belong to dangerous animals, she could sleep in mother's arms.

It was long after dark before they made camp that night. A lunch of sandwiches and oranges, eaten as they journeyed along, saved them the trouble of sitting up late to eat. The wagon was unloaded, the bed made in the wagon bottom, and the mosquito netting attached to the awning poles.

But the native workers got their hot supper; and after it was over sat around the fire talking and singing till nearly midnight. Finally, they, too, became weary, rolled up in the blankets, head and all, to keep out the mosquitoes, and went to sleep.

27
At the Village

About ten o'clock next morning, the m1ss1on party reached the first village that they intended to visit. Here one of the former students from the mission was teaching a school. The party had traveled thirty-eight miles in a day and a half. A train could have made the distance in about an hour. But the only railway in the whole country did not pass anywhere near this village. Daddy said they should be thankful for these long rides in the wagon that gave them all time to rest and think. The camp wagon drew up under a wild fig tree.

Nearly all the people in the village came out to see the strangers. There were about thirty dogs, gaunt and thin, seemingly too scared or too languid to bark. There were scores of slim, half-naked little children, who stood as straight as arrows. The women came running out of their huts with their babies on their backs, and old men followed, carrying spears or sticks.

While breakfast was being prepared, daddy went with Peter to see the headman of the village. The people lingered about the camp to have a few words with the strangers. Mother couldn't understand much of what was said; and Samuel didn't know English well enough yet to explain it to her. But in spite of that, they enjoyed the visit. When Oleta took off her hat, the people shouted with delight at sight of her long curls. Little picanins peeked shyly out from behind their mothers' buckskin skirts.

They were much interested in Baby Rose. They would touch the doll's mouth and nose, then point to their own.

How they laughed and chattered to one another in their queer-sounding language! When Oleta turned Baby Rose over and made her say "Mama," they exclaimed in astonishment, "Weh! Weh! Weh!"

After a time daddy returned with Peter and the teacher. The headman was also with them. He greeted Oleta and her mother, and made them a present of a basket of eggs. Daddy gave him a few oranges and a handful of dates.

Before breakfast was finished the gong sounded for school. The gong, which hung from a tree in front of the schoolhouse, was an iron disk taken from an old mission plow. The clapper was a piece of iron attached to it by a cord. In response to the gong, boys and girls came from the surrounding huts. The big people came too. They all wanted to hear what the missionary had to say.

An ant hill makes a fine place from which these boys can watch the missionary coming to their village

The schoolhouse was a little, square building made of poles, plastered inside and out with mud. It had a grass roof. There were two openings for doors, five little, square window-holes, and a floor of hard, smooth earth.

The people came in and sat down on the floor. The teacher brought four low stools for the missionary's family and Peter to sit on. These stools had been whittled from blocks of wood by the boys who were attending the school.

When all were ready, the teacher led them in singing. The people knew the hymns well, and sang as if they meant every word and really loved to sing. After prayer, the missionary talked to the people. He would speak one sentence in English, then wait for Peter to interpret it in the Chitonga language. Then he would say another sentence. It took a long time to say a very little. When he had finished, he told all those who were not students in the school to go to their homes, and come back again at sunset.

28
Going to School in Africa

"Now," said daddy to the teacher as soon as the pupils were again quiet, "you go ahead and have school just as you always do, and we will listen."

The meeting had already been opened with prayer and singing, so the teacher proceeded to call the roll. He then told the story of Baby Moses in the basket boat, and had the children repeat all the memory verses they had learned since the beginning of the month. After this, two boys passed the slates and hung up the reading chart, and the beginners read their lesson. The teacher pointed with a stick to the words, and the class shouted them in concert. But some seemed to be reading from their toes, and others from the poles in the roof. They had gone over that chart so many times that they knew the lesson by heart.

While the chart class was reciting, the primer class was reading a new lesson. Only a few of the pupils had books, so they sat in groups like Sabbath school classes, and read out loud. Those who knew the lesson well helped the others. Another class was reading from a book of Bible stories; and a still more advanced class was reading from Testaments. They had no Bibles in their own language, but used New Testaments that had been translated into a language so nearly like their own that they could understand it.

After the reading lessons were over, those who had slates printed the new words. The beginners made their letters on the ground out of corn kernels. When it came time for spelling, the teacher sent the classes out under the trees. He chose a boy from each class to hear the others spell.

On the schoolhouse floor, among the children and big boys, sat mothers with babies on their backs. They, too, were learning to read and write and count. Once in a while a baby would cry. Its mother would stand up and sway her body gently to and fro to quiet the little one, holding her book in her hand, and continuing her study at the same time. When the baby became tired of crying, she would sit down again as if nothing had happened, and pay no further attention to the child.

The arithmetic hour came after recess. On their slates the advanced classes worked examples in addition and multiplication from the blackboard. The beginners went out with the teacher under the trees, and counted clay oxen. Oleta joined this class.

The teacher marked out a cattle-kraal by laying sticks on the ground; and a little new girl put the oxen into the kraal one at a time, while the other

The mission school teacher uses old gasoline cans on an ox sled to bring his water from the river

children counted, first in their own language, and then in English, "one, two, three, four, five, six, seven, eight, nine, ten." Two of the boys in the beginners' class were larger than the teacher himself. The pupils were not playing and whispering, but were paying good attention, and all seemed anxious to learn. After a time the teacher went inside to correct slates, leaving daddy to continue the counting lesson under the trees.

School lasted about three hours, and then the children went home, laughing and chattering, to help fetch wood and water, and to tell their smaller brothers and sisters about the queer little white girl who had visited them that day.

After school, daddy and the teacher had a conference. The teacher needed more chalk, and slate pencils, and Testaments, and primers. All of these were provided, except the primers. The schools would have to wait about three months before another set of primers could be printed.

There was a broad smile on the teacher's face when daddy asked if he would like a new picture roll. Daddy went to the wagon for the roll. It was not really a new one, having done service already in several schools. Its edges were ragged, and its pages had been patched with brown paper in many places. But it was new to the children in this village.

The teacher went into his hut and took from a kerosene tin that hung by a wire from the roof a picture roll wrapped carefully in blue calico. The calico had protected it from dust, and the kerosene tin suspended from the roof had kept it away from the white ants that would have been glad to have feasted upon it.

"Do you know where we get these picture rolls?" the missionary asked.

"I should like to know," replied the teacher.

"The little children in the Sabbath schools in America send them to us.

"Then, will you tell the children that we say to them, 'We wish to thank you for the beautiful pictures. They bring many children to our Sabbath school. Will you please continue to send them?'"

29
The Meeting

In the evening, when the sun was set, the teacher and his wife brought branches and logs and piled them high on the camp fire. Oleta's father got out the little phonograph that they had brought in the camp wagon, and began playing hymns. Before the first hymn was finished, the people had begun to gather about the brightly burning fire.

There were exclamations of surprise and wonder as they seated themselves at a safe distance from the music box. "What are they saying?" Oleta asked of Peter.

"They say, 'It must be a very small man inside that box, but that he has a large voice.'"

How those people made the fields and woods ring with their singing that night! After Daddy had spoken to them a few minutes, he asked the people to give their testimonies. Peter very softly repeated in English what they said, so that mother could understand it better.

One testimony was like this: "We are so glad that God has sent us the light. Once we were foolish. We were great sinners. Now we know the way of life. Once we feared the spirits of dead people. Now we know that they are asleep and cannot hurt us. We pray that God may bless the missionaries, and help them to send the light quickly to our brothers who are still in darkness."

One said: "I love Jesus, because He takes away my sin, and makes my heart clean, and makes me wish to be good."

Oleta sat in her mother's lap, wrapped snugly in daddy's rain coat to keep away from the mosquitoes.

She had to sit so still that she soon fell asleep, and was tucked safely into bed under the mosquito netting in the wagon.

Anyone who had chanced to peek into the school house that night after the services were over would have seen an interesting group of people sitting on low stools, around a dimly burning lantern, in a corner of the school house. The headman of the village was the central figure. The missionary and his interpreter and the school teacher were also there.

The headman wished to be baptized at the next camp meeting. He had brought to the missionary some of the magic medicine and charms that he had given up using. There was a snakeskin bag filled with medicine powders, which he wore on his breast and which was supposed to keep his people loyal and peaceful. He also brought a bracelet made from the bark of a medicine tree twined together with the legs and wings of certain insects. This was supposed to bring him good luck and prosperity. "These foolish things,—I give them to you. I will never look upon them again, for Jesus is my strong helper and friend. The war drum I will keep; but it shall never again call my people to drunken feasts. It shall be used only to signal messages to neighboring villages. I and my people want to be Christians."

The teacher then told how God had blessed the people of the village in healing their sick, and in sending them rain in answer to prayer. The men were giving up their tobacco, and the women were throwing away their snuff.

Daddy said it was worth coming all the way from America just to hear of the wonderful things God was doing for the people of Africa.

30
At Malambo's Village

The next day the missionary party went on to another village. Here the people came out to meet them in groups. They seemed sick and tired, and their eyes looked red. This was Malambo's village, where the big dance had been going on for three days. There was no Christian school here. Some of the people had sores on their legs. There were many sick babies. And there was no one to help them.

Daddy got out his medicine box and treated them.

Malambo brought a fowl for a present; and Ba-ka-Milupi, his wife, came with a jar of beer. Peter explained that the missionaries did not drink beer. He asked Malambo to send some of his boys to fetch water.

The water was muddy and brown, but it was the best to be found. Samuel filled the big tin can with it, and boiled it over the camp fire. When it was cool, he poured it into the canvas water-bags and hung them on the limb of a tree.

Some of these people had never seen a white woman or child before. They thought them very queer, and supposed that they must have lost their outside skin. At first they thought that Baby Rose was some sort of a charm, until mother tied the doll on Oleta's back to show them that it was her play baby.

All the children in the village gathered to see Oleta and her Teddy bear

Oleta did not quite like having so many of the children so close to her. Some of them were not very clean. So she made Teddy growl and pretend to chase them. Of course, she did the growling herself; but they thought it was the Teddy bear and ran away in fright. However, they were soon back again, peering into the wagon, and trying to see what was in the food box every time the lid was opened.

Three little boys stood quite close, watching in wonder as Samuel unpacked the shining pots and pans and opened the tins of food. Their eyes were so big, and their bodies so thin! "Mummie, can't I please give them some cookies?"

"If you do, you will have to give some to all these other children too."

"Oh, do let me, Mummie."

"What shall I do?" mother thought to herself. "There must be eighty or a hundred children in a village of this size."

Finally she yielded to Oleta's entreaties, and the cookies were passed out to the children standing around. A dozen or more little children each held out two hands to receive a cooky. To have held out one hand only would have been a sign of ingratitude. It would have shown that the gift was not appreciated.

Oleta expected to see the children eat the cookies. But not a child took a bite. They all scampered to their huts to divide the curious tid-bits with their brothers and sisters. "I wish white children were always as generous as these little African boys and girls," mother remarked.

But before long the children came trooping back with their brothers and sisters and mothers and grand mothers. They stood at a little distance and looked and looked. A woman held out her hands for a present, and mother gave her a little salt. Then the others all held out their hands, and she had to give them a little all around.

31
Oleta Goes Visiting

In the afternoon, the missionary family went with Peter to see Malambo's hut. Outside, in the shade of the wide veranda of thatch, his wife was grinding kafir corn between two flat stones. Nzala sat on the ground by the door with her feet crossed in front of her, making rings of soft clay. She was stacking the rings one upon another. *"Ko bola, kasimbi* [Come here, little maiden]," Peter said, "and speak to the white child. What is your name?"

"Nzala," the little girl replied.

"Nzala means hunger. She must have been born in a famine year," Peter explained.

"May we enter?" Peter asked of the mother.

Ba-ka-Milupi led the way inside, and brought stools. While daddy and Peter exchanged a few words with Malambo, Oleta and her mother looked around.

The hut was divided into two rooms by a partition of corn stalks, which reached a little higher than a man's head. Against the partition stood a row of big jars, containing various kinds of food, such as dried pumpkin leaves, *mealie* meal, peanuts, dried fish, and kafir corn.

A few axes and spears stood near the door, ready for use in case any wild beast should come prowling around the village. The broom, which had just been picked from a tree, stood in the corner of the room. It consisted of a few leafy branches tied together with strips of bark. By the wall, opposite the partition, a pot of water, sup ported by three fire-stones, was steaming over a slowly burning fire. The ends of the burning sticks had fallen from the fire and lay scattered about.

"Where is the chimney?" asked mother. Peter pointed to the small window-hole.

"And do they keep a fire all the time?" she questioned again.

"Nearly all the time," Peter answered. "Otherwise, they fear the family ghosts would become uncomfortable and flee away."

Along the wall opposite the door was a long, low plat form of mud. It was covered with mats and skins. In the daytime it was used as a sort of sofa where visitors might sit; and at night it served as grandma's bed. The children slept on the floor. Their mats were neatly rolled up and lying against the wall.

Another higher, but smaller, mud platform served as a cupboard, where bowls and jars of food could be placed out of reach of the dogs and chickens. Several grass baskets, filled with trinkets, hung from wooden pegs on the wall. The pegs had been built into the wall when the mud plaster was applied.

Peter asked permission to step into the second room. There they saw a real frame bed. The frame was built of saplings and was supported on four short, crotched sticks planted in the dirt floor. Split poles were laid cross wise over the frame and tied on with strips of hide. Several layers of skins covered the bed.

Two large wooden pegs answered the purpose of a wardrobe. On one hung Ba-ka-Milupi's leopard-skin skirt. On the other hung Malambo's long, brown over coat. These garments were worn at the big feasts and other special occasions.

Oleta's father showed the village boys how to set the dry grass on fire with a reading glass

Oleta pointed to a little horn that hung on the center pole. "May I see what's inside?" she asked.

"This is a *duiker* horn," Peter replied. "It is filled with medicine that is supposed to protect the family from harm." Daddy told Peter to ask Malambo more about the horn. Malambo explained, and Peter translated.

"Malambo says that this is a very powerful charm. He gave the doctor a heifer and two goats for it. As long as it hangs there, no harm can come to any one in the hut, for it will make the hut invisible to any spirits who may be planning mischief. They will pass by without seeing anything here, and will go on till they come to a hut that is unprotected. It never fails, 'unless,' as Malambo says, 'a more powerful charm is used against us by an enemy.'"

"And does Malambo really believe this?" mother asked.

"He believes it," Peter replied. "All his people believe it. They know no better."

There was another medicine horn tucked under the bed; and still another hung over the doorway. There were also little ones for various members of the family to wear around their necks.

A little skin bag, dangling from a wisp of grass that stuck out over the cornstalk partition, attracted Oleta's attention. Peter asked Malambo to tell him about it; and then Peter explained to the others. "It is made of the skin of a wild cat. It is thought to be dangerous for the mother of a little baby to be out at night; for if a wild cat should happen to cross her pathway, it is feared the baby will have convulsions. When Ba-ka-Milupi goes out at night, she always fastens the cat-skin bag to the baby-blanket to ward off this danger."

32
Work in the Village

Nzala was still working with the clay when the visitors came out of the hut. Her stack of rings was complete; and she was beginning to press them together and to smooth the sides. The bottom rings were small, the center ones larger, and the top ones smaller again.

"She is making a cooking pot," Peter explained. "When she has pressed the rings together, she will sprinkle the pot with water, and then smooth it again with that flat piece of bone she holds in her hand. When the pot is finished, she will set it in the shade for two days, mark patterns on the outside, and then dry it in the sun.

"She and her mother will make many pots of different sizes. When they are all thoroughly dry, they will dig a hole in the ground, lay the pots in the hole, and build a fire of bark over them. The burning makes the pots strong and water-tight."

Much interesting work was going on in the village. One man was whittling a spear handle. Others were weaving mats of reeds. Another was mending a drum. A group of women were weaving baskets of palm-leaf strips and grass.

Two young men were softening skins. "This kind of work," Peter said, "takes much time and patience. First the skins have to be pegged out and dried. Then they must be rubbed for a long time on the smooth side with a stone or lump of hard clay. After this, they are rubbed between the hands with a little butter until they are very soft. Then the men sew them into skirts for the women to wear."

"They certainly are good seamstresses," mother remarked, examining a garment. "The sewing is neat and even, and the stitches -how tiny they are!"

"What's that big thing?" Oleta asked, spying a large calabash standing by one of the huts.

"That's the churn," Peter told her. "The milk left each morning is poured into the churn and left to sour. At night, while the men sit around the fire, they shake the churn till the butter comes. Then they remove this wooden stopper in the top and pour the buttermilk off. "The next morning more milk is poured into the churn over the butter that is already in it, and it is set to sour, and churned again. This is continued many days, until the churn is filled with butter. Then the wooden stopper in the bottom of the churn is removed. The man who is doing the churning places his lips over the small hole in the bottom, and blows the butter out through the top.

"It is then melted over the fire, and the pure fat is poured into a small calabash and tied to one of the rafters of the hut, to be used later as a toilet article."

"You have certainly made our visit interesting, Peter," mother said. Then she added, "But it seems to me your people have things turned around. The women hoe the gardens, carry wood and water, and manufacture the pots and dishes; while the men do the sewing and churning and mat weaving, which seems to be easy work."

"No, madam, I think the work is well divided. Is not the work of gathering poles more difficult than cutting grass? Would you choose to spear the game, while your husband sat quietly by the river, watching fish swim into the basket traps?"

"There are evidently two sides to every question, Peter. Here we are at our camp."

33
Grandma's Question Answered

Nearly the whole village came out that night to listen to the music and singing, and to hear the word that the white man would speak. He told them that *Leza,* who had made heaven and earth, had spoken to them. "His words are in this book," he said, holding the Bible up so that all might see it in the firelight. "I am going to read some of these words to you tonight." Then he read verses in the Bible that told of God's love for man.

When, at the opening of the meeting, the missionary asked them to kneel while he spoke to the great God, the people thought that they should put their faces to the ground. The babies on the backs of their mothers were not used to this strange position, and set up a chorus of objections. One by one, the mothers got up and ran away toward the huts, to quiet their little ones and to readjust the baby-blankets.

For the first time these people heard that it is not God who sends the trouble that we see in this world, but that it is a rebel angel, called Satan. They heard about Jesus, God's only Son, who gave His life to redeem them, that they might live forever. They learned that if they wished to become children of God they must seek to learn and obey His words which were written in the Book. They were told for the first time that they them selves could speak to the great God, and that He would hear and help them.

"You need not fear the spirits of the dead," he told them. "They have no more power to hurt you than does a sleeping child." Then he opened his Bible again, and read words that God himself had spoken, showing that the dead are asleep, that they know nothing, and can neither help nor hurt those who are living on the earth.

"The spirits that bring evil upon men," he said, "are Satan and his wicked angels. But Jesus has met these rebels in battle, and has overcome them all. If you will make Jesus your friend, He will be your helper. Then you will have nothing in the world to fear, not even death itself. For if you turn away from following Satan, and choose to obey God, He will give you eternal life. Jesus will come again to this earth to save His people and take them away from all this trouble. At that time all the dead shall live again. Satan and his rebel angels will be destroyed. And there will be no more trouble or sorrow or death forever."

Malambo was present, with all of his wives and children. They listened motionless and silent. Only once did Grandma take her eyes off the missionary's face, and that was to wipe away the tears that she could not keep back. So, after all, the great God was her friend. He loved her and her poor people. It seemed too wonderful to believe.

And He was not the one who had sent her all her trouble. Only the night before, she had said to the children: "The old woman never found God; no one has ever found Him." But while she had been speaking, the missionaries were on their way to her, coming with a message of love and hope.

God had sent them from a far country that she and her people might hear His words: "God so loved the world that He gave His only-begotten Son, that whosoever believeth in Him, should not perish, but have everlasting life." She repeated over and over: "God so loved the world that He gave His Son." Something in her heart told her that the words were true, and she felt a strange, sweet joy in believing them.

All that the poor old woman ever knew of Jesus, she heard that night. In the morning the missionaries went on to other villages; and before they visited Malambo's people again she was dead. But from what she learned in those few moments, she knew that Jesus was the very friend she needed. From that day she was often seen sitting on her stool in the corner of the hut, talking to her unseen Friend.

After the missionary finished speaking, Malambo rose and said, "These are good words. I hope all the young men will follow this good way. But I am too old to change. I cannot give up my old ways."

The others said nothing, nor did they show by any expression of the face what their thoughts were. But the people gathered in little groups around their various fires in the compound and talked it all over. When the night was half gone, and the light of the camp fires had nearly died out, some of the men could still be heard talking.

34
Choma Goes to the Mission

Choma was determined to go back to the school with the missionaries. But Malambo would not give consent to this. He said to the missionary, "Now the white man has come to our country; we are not permitted to buy slaves; and he even seeks to take away our own children. Choma must stay to herd my cattle and hoe my garden."

"If your son comes to the mission," answered the missionary, "he will become a wise man. Then he can return and teach you and the people of your village great wisdom." But Malambo still refused.

Choma did not give up his purpose, however. He stayed to talk with the teachers that night, and learned all he could about the mission and the way to get to it.

He had been making some palm-fiber rope, and had just finished three lengths. It had taken him several days to make it. At first he had pounded the palm leaves with a stone until the pulp was loosened from the fibers. Then he washed the fibers, and twisted them into rope by rubbing them between the palm of his hand and his leg.

In the morning, Choma brought his rope and showed it to the teachers. The missionary needed rope, and gave Choma a shilling for the three pieces.

Choma goes away to school

At once Choma brought the shilling to the teachers. "I wish to buy that *mealie* bag [grain sack]."

"Why do you want it?" they asked.

"You told me that at the mission the boys wear clothes," he replied. "I have none. My father will not give me even a buckskin to wear, because he does not wish me to go. If I cannot go with you, I shall run away from my home, and come to the mission.

"But grandma is pleading with father for me, also my mother is begging him to let me go. They are saying that their great new spirit-friend Jesus will make father willing. They wish me to go to the mission and learn about God, that I can teach my people more. When I go I shall cover my body with the *mealie*-bag."

And so it happened that while the missionary was preaching in the next village, a lad dressed in a grain sack, with a piece of bark string tied around his waist, joined the group of listeners. He carried a calabash of meal on a stick over his shoulder. He was hot and tired, for he had run all the way.

Choma's father had at last consented. The boy was happy. He would trudge along with the cook and leader boy from village to village until they returned to the mission. *Choma was going to school.*

Experiences at the Mission
35
Home Again

Late one night, after an absence of three weeks, the mission wagon rumbled into the compound (the boys' sleeping quarters) and on past it to Oleta's house. Daddy blew a blast on his police whistle. The houseboy came up, unlocked the house, and made the beds. Mother undressed her sleepy little girl, and then started to unpack the suitcase.

When she looked into the sitting room, what a sight she saw! The white ants had come up through a crack in the cement floor, and had eaten great holes in the linoleum. She sat down on the sofa, her face full of dismay. She could not speak, tears were too near the surface. "We don't have to look at the floor," said daddy cheerfully.

"No," replied mother, with a queer, little, puckery smile. "Let's look at the ceiling. [The ceiling was all stained where water had dripped through the old thatch.] And at the woodwork and walls," she added. White ants had been industriously working for years, eating out the door and window casements, until they were nearly falling to pieces.

Daddy took mother by the arm and led her out to the veranda. He held the lantern over the little bed where Oleta slept. "My dear, look at those rosy cheeks; listen to that even breathing,- never mind the linoleum."

"Yes! yes!" Tears came into mother's eyes at last, but they were tears of thankfulness.

Daddy hung the lantern in its customary place on a wire from the veranda ceiling. It had long done service as a hanging lamp. The evening was cool, with a suggestion of rain in it. They sat down and talked about the early days, when missionaries first came to the country. There were no comfortable houses then, no gardens nor orange orchards, and very poor means of protection from the fever-carrying mosquitoes. Down in the field was a little cemetery, with graves in it. How foolish it seemed to care so much for a piece of linoleum!

Some of the boys at the compound were sitting around the fire singing the old familiar songs that are sung by Christians the world over. "I wonder how many people are singing those same songs tonight and in how many different languages," suggested daddy. "Listen, mother, just hear Petros sing! What a clear voice he has! You can hear his voice above all the others. Do you remember the day when Petros came to us? What a dirty, ragged little fellow he was! That was only a few months ago, the first week after we arrived at the mission. And now he is singing, 'When the roll is called up yonder, I'll be there.' "

Daddy had been scanning the reports of the General Conference in a late *Review.* He read, "Let us close this service by singing Number 865, 'When the roll is called up yonder.' "

"Wouldn't you like to be there, listening to that congregation sing that song?"

"Wouldn't I! Oh, wouldn't I!" And then, after a pause: "But we'd rather be here, listening to our boys sing it, wouldn't we?"

36
Choma's First Night

As soon as the mission wagon had been unloaded and the oxen outspanned, the leader boy took Choma to the compound. But the compound was full. Where could he sleep? The two boys looked into one room after another. Every room was full of beds, and every bed was occupied. Besides this, boys were sleeping between the beds, on grain sacks spread on the floor.

At last they came to a room that seemed to have a few inches of floor space to spare. The leader boy introduced the newcomer. The two boys sleeping nearest the door edged over a little, and Choma lay down on the floor beside them. They stretched the blanket out, so as to partly cover their guest. Toward morning, when the night became chilly, they would all wrap up in the sacks on which they were sleeping.

Choma's new companions tried to make him feel comfortable. "We must work for awhile, and then we shall get blankets," they told him; "the mission will give them to us." Choma did not need comforting. True, he felt a little strange. This was the first time that he had ever been away from home. But he was so happy to be at the mission that other things mattered little. And although not altogether comfortable—the blanket did not reach far enough toward his side—he was too tired and sleepy to stay awake long.

37
Choma's First Day

A little before sunrise the big bell rang. About ten minutes later the chapel gong sounded, and all the boys gathered in the schoolhouse. They had a short chapel service, and then went outside to have their work assigned for the morning.

The house boys and the kitchen boys for the three houses had already gone to their tasks. The houseboys did the washing and ironing and sweeping and bed making. The kitchen boys made fires, washed dishes, prepared the vegetables for dinner, set the tables, and scrubbed the kitchens.

Three boys were appointed to cook and wash dishes for the students at the compound, and two others to gather greens for the relish, to eat with the porridge. There were garden boys, who planted and weeded the gardens, and sprinkled them with water from the spring. The poultry boy cared for the fowls and gathered the eggs.

There were seven herd boys, who had to take the oxen and cows and calves to pasture, and do the milking and separating of the cream. The wood boys gathered bundles of firewood, tied them with bark strips to poles, and carried them home on their shoulders. The water boys carried buckets of water from the well to the mission homes and to the compound.

All this work had been assigned at the beginning of the month; so these boys went at once to their regular work. The others lined up, and the farm manager looked along the line, assigning to each boy his work for the day. Choma took his place with the others. Two boys were selected to run the *mealie* grinder, and two to gather oranges for shipping. The rest were sent in gangs, some to make bricks, others to cultivate the orchard, and still others to mow grass around the buildings.

When the manager came to Choma, he asked, "What is your name?" But Choma was afraid to tell his own name. To do so, he believed, would bring a curse upon him. He had never once, in all his life, repeated his own name. It seemed too sacred for him to pronounce, be cause it had belonged to his mother's grandfather, and had been given him by a special ceremony.

When Choma was born, his parents thought that the spirit of one of his ancestors had come to live in their baby. They wished to find out whose spirit it was, so they could name their baby after him. So, while he was still a baby, the witch doctor was called in, and the names of his ancestors were repeated very slowly.

Experiences at the Mission

When they came to the name of the mother's grandfather, Choma, the baby waved his arms in an excited way, and began to cry for food. They thought that the spirit inside the baby had recognized his old name, the name by which he had been called when he lived on the earth before. Choma was taught that the spirit of his great-grandfather, Choma, would be his helping spirit throughout his life.

Choma had a nickname. It was *Mukadi,* and meant, "The fierce, brave one." But for Choma to have given this name would have sounded boastful. So he turned to one of the other boys, and asked him to tell the *m'fundisi* (missionary) his name. One of the other boys might repeat the name Choma without any harm. The name was finally written down, and Choma was sent to lead the oxen for one of the young men who had to cultivate.

Work continued till breakfast time at half past nine. After breakfast, during the hottest part of the day, the boys went to school. After school, when it was cooler, they worked again until time for the evening meal. After this came the night school.

Choma could not begin day school at once. He must first work for four months to earn clothes and blankets. But in the evening, when his work was finished, he would slip into the night school and listen to the other boys recite. In this way he learned much.

Many of the schoolboys helped make the bricks for the new building

38
Choma's First Sabbath

No school was held on Fridays, and there was never work on Friday afternoons. This gave the boys time to clean out their rooms, and to go to the river for baths. They washed their shirts and trousers, and spread them on the grass or hung them on bushes while they took their baths.

Choma had no clothes to wash. He did not like to go to church in his *mealie* bag suit. One of the boys who had been at the mission long enough to earn a respectable outfit, offered to sell Choma his old trousers and the remains of a shirt for sixpence. Still Choma did not know what to do, for he had no sixpence.

But one of his new friends explained that there were little jobs on Friday afternoons, such as watering seeds, running errands, or cleaning the yard. If he stood around near the pump, where one of the *afundisi* (missionaries) could see that he was waiting for work, he might have a chance to earn a threepence now and again. So he promised sixpence for the old shirt and trousers, to be paid as soon as he could earn it, and took possession of his newly acquired wardrobe.

Another prosperous boy dug out a piece of string from under his corn husk pillow, where he had carefully hidden it, and generously offered it to Choma, who fastened the parts of his shirt together over his shoulders with a lace work of string, and tied up the largest holes in the trousers, according to the accepted style. Before the sun was set and the gong sounded for vespers, Choma was ready to go with the others to the chapel.

On the Sabbath day many people came to the mission from the heathen villages round about. There were three meetings during the day. The first one was the baptismal class. Here they learned how to live the Christian life. They also committed to memory Bible verses that had been translated into their language and that would especially help them. Often when drunken feasts were held in the villages, these Christian converts would go away by themselves and spend the time singing and repeating the Bible verses they had learned in the baptismal class.

When Sabbath school time came, the little chapel was packed. All the wooden benches were filled, and picanins were sitting so close together on the floor that there was scarcely room to pass between them. Most of the classes went outside and sat down on the ground to recite.

After the preaching service, the students separated into groups and went out into the surrounding villages to hold meetings. Choma joined a group of students. The meeting was led by one of the student teachers. He hung a picture roll on a tree, and told several Bible stories. Then he pleaded with the people to give their hearts to Jesus. The students who had come with him helped in the singing and gave their testimony.

About two hundred hymns had been translated and printed in a little book. Wherever the student teachers held meetings, they taught the people these beautiful hymns. And how the people did love to sing! As the native teachers often said, "When these heathen people begin singing gospel songs, the evil spirits flee away, and the angels of God come near."

"Yes," the missionary would reply, "that is true everywhere in the world."

39
Choma in Trouble

At the beginning of the month, when work was changed, Choma was made herd boy. There were two older boys appointed to care for the cows, and two for the oxen. Choma's part of the work was to tend the calves. Early in the morning he drove them away to pasture. Twice every day he took them to the river to drink. All through the hot days he watched them, and trudged along behind them over hills and fields while they nibbled grass.

Sometimes on a hot afternoon a sudden gust of wind would come up. The clouds would gather, and before Choma could get his slow-moving herd into the shelter of a tree, the rain would be falling in torrents. Choma liked the cool rain. But the lightning and thunder terrified him. He felt sure God was angry. He would crouch be hind a bush, and put his hands over his face, and pray to his helping spirit to protect him. When his father s sister was alive, she had loved Choma, and Choma had loved her. He now often asked her spirit to remember him in his danger.

He believed the words that he had heard the teachers in the night school read from the Bible. But it seemed so hard to realize that the great God loved him and would hear him pray. Sometime, perhaps, when he knew as much as his teachers did about God, he would not fear to pray to Him.

Herd boys amuse themselves playing a little musical instrument that has keys like piano keys

Choma was faithful, and took good care of the calves. All went well for three weeks. Then something dreadful happened. There was no night school on Thursday evenings, so the boys usually played games in the evening.

One night, when the moon was full, they played very late.

The next day was hot and sultry, and the clouds hung low. As Choma trudged over the fields with his calves, he became so tired that he sat down under a tree to rest. Soon he was fast asleep. While he slept, the calves wandered off. They went down to the stream for a drink. On the other side of the stream there was a spot of green. The calves had not seen anything so tempting for many a day. Soon they were in the mission garden, crunching cabbages and lettuce and spinach. All of a sudden Choma awoke. He looked for the calves, but could not find them.

That afternoon Choma was called into the director's office. The director was a kind *m'fundisi* who loved his boys a great deal more than he loved the calves and the garden. But Choma must learn to put work before play. Because of his carelessness, the calves had done much damage. Choma was forbidden to play after sunset for a time and had to work five months instead of four before beginning his regular school.

40
Choma Acquires Property

A year had passed since Choma first came to the mission. He had finished his primer, and was reading in the book of Bible stories. He had also learned to work. He had been herd boy, and wood boy, and water boy, and yard boy. He had planted and hoed and harvested *mealies* according to the white man's method. He had taken his turn at sweeping the school yard and washing windows. He had learned to keep his clothes clean and mended. He had been taught that it is wrong to lie and steal and fight, and had learned to pray directly to God.

He had a bed of his own now, having made it himself of poles and cowhide strips. And he had built a little bookshelf out of kerosene boxes. Last of all, from a cracker box he had manufactured a trunk with hinges and lock on it. It wasn't very large, to be sure; but it held all his possessions, from his new Sabbath shirt to an empty shoe-blacking tin, a rusty knife, and a few bits of slate.

He was also acquiring some wealth. One day he bought a little white chick with a broken leg. Every morning the compound cook gave the scrapings of one of the porridge pots to feed to the chick. In return for this favor, Choma washed the pot. The chick thrived, and his leg mended. He grew to be a fine rooster. When he was half grown, Choma traded him for a small hen.

He made a nest of mud under his bed, lined it with dry grass, and set his hen on half a dozen eggs. When the chicks began to scratch for themselves, they became such a nuisance around the compound that he had to sell them. But he increased the pile of sixpences in his little trunk.

41
In the Kitchen

The missionary was losing all his old teachers from the school. One by one they were being sent out to teach village schools. He decided it was time to start a new morning class for training teachers. These new student teachers would stay in the training class for a year. They would help with the teaching at the mission school and in the schools near by until they, in their turn, were called to go out and start new schools in the villages.

Oleta's mother had to find a new kitchen boy while she let her old kitchen boy join the teachers' class. She decided she would like Choma. Choma was pleased when they sent him up to the house to work for the "missis."

She showed him how to peel the vegetables, and set the table, and sweep and scrub the floor. He was very slow at first. It took a lot of patience to show him how to do the work, and then to wait for him to do it. But he did his best, and learned fast.

One morning, when the family sat down to breakfast, they found the plates sticky. Daddy had to wait while mother and Oleta gathered them up and washed them.

Mother could not find out the reason. Every time she stepped into the kitchen to discover the secret, she found Choma washing and rinsing his

If these boys had brought the water as they should,
Choma would not have left the dishes dirty

dishes as she had shown him, and the towels were clean. Just why the dishes had been so sticky that one day remained a puzzle.

One afternoon she went to get a cup from the cupboard.

Choma was washing dishes, but not in the usual way. This time he had very little water in the bottom of his pan, and no rinse water at all. He was wringing his dish cloth out of the water and wiping the dirty plates with it.

"Chibiabi [bad]." she said. And to her question, "Why are you doing so?" the boy replied, "Water, he small."

Sure enough, the teakettle was empty; and the water drum that stood on the veranda outside the kitchen door was empty too. The water boys had been slow with their work.

Mother handed Choma a bucket, and pointed down the path toward the pump. *"Ko leta menda* [bring water]." she said.

Very slowly Choma picked up the bucket. Very slowly he marched out of the kitchen. He looked as if he would like to say, "The idea of going so far for water, just so the dishes can shine!" And he felt it to be a terrible disgrace for a kitchen boy to carry water.

42
Tempted

On Choma's first Sabbath at the mission, he entered the hearers' class. At the end of six months he was promoted to the baptismal class. He had now been in this class for nearly a year, and was looking forward to the next camp meeting, when he expected to be baptized. He had chosen Paul for his Christian name. But as there were several other students at the mission by that name, he was called Paul Choma.

Paul Choma had many battles with his temper. He did not always understand the ways of the white man. Sometimes he would become angry when asked to do his work over again. Why was it necessary to be so particular about a little bit of dirt? But he was always sorry afterwards, and would say in his newly acquired English phrases, "I make mistake; I not speak so again."

One morning the missionary's wife noticed that the soap in the kitchen was not lasting as long as it should. She determined to learn the reason, if possible. So when Choma called for a new cake of soap, she buried a piece of a match in the end of it before handing it to him. A few hours later she looked for the cake of soap. The new cake was gone from the shelf, and a half-used one was in its place.

"Choma, where is the cake of soap that I gave you this morning?" she asked.

"Yes, missis," he answered, handing her the small piece from the shelf.

"This is not the piece I gave you today."

"Yes, missis, I washed the dish towels."

"But, didn't I tell you to use the soap ends in the tin for the dish towels?" she questioned him.

"Missis, I did forget."

The missionary's wife took up the piece of soap and examined it. "Choma," she said, "this is not the piece of soap I gave you. You must bring me the other piece."

That night, while all the boys were in school, she slipped into Choma's room at the compound and opened his trunk. She had given him the lock for his trunk, and had kept one key for herself.

In the corner of his box she saw three new cakes of soap. In one of the cakes she found the buried match. She pressed the soap together again over the match, put it back, and closed and locked the trunk.

What should she do? Poor Choma! She felt so sorry for him! He had been planning a visit home, and had been saving money to buy a blanket to take to his mother. He could sell the three cakes of soap in the village for ninepence.

The next morning the cake of soap with the match in it was on the kitchen shelf. Choma explained that he had left it outside by the wash box when he washed the dish towels, and had forgotten about it.

The "missis" looked at him. "You are telling me a lie," she said. He denied it. But she continued, "It is noble of you to buy a blanket for your mother, if you earn the money for it honestly. But to steal soap and hide it in your trunk that you may sell it—that is a sin. And to lie about it is another sin. You have broken two of God's commandments; and unless you confess what you have done, and make things right, you cannot be baptized with the other students at camp-meeting time."

Choma had never realized before that it was really a sin to take a small cake of soap. It was such a little thing. The white man had so much. He had so little. He knew that to lie was not the Christian way. But from babyhood he had been taught to do so. It was part of the religion of his people. He must lie in order to outwit the spirits who were constantly trying to harm him. And now, though he had learned that it was wrong, the old habit still clung to him.

For a time Choma thought that he would rather not be baptized than to confess himself a thief. After a terrible struggle, he told the whole story, and brought back the two remaining pieces of soap. That was the last time Choma was known to steal.

43
The Meeting Camp

It was camp-meeting time at the mission. Everybody was astir. The boys at the compound were cleaning out their rooms and washing their blankets. One group was cleaning the chapel and washing the windows. Another was raking the grounds and sweeping the paths. Still other groups were gathering bundles of thatch grass from the fields with which to build two large shelters for the people who were coming. These shelters consisted of four walls of poles and grass, without roof. They kept off the wind, and there was no danger of rain at this time of the year.

Thursday night, the first company arrived. Far in the distance they could be heard singing, in their own beautiful language, "Dare to be a Daniel." Soon they came in sight, traveling single file along the path through the tall grass. They were the Christian converts from teacher David's school.

They had spent two days on the journey, camping along the way. The women carried babies on their backs and bundles on their heads. The men and boys carried blanket rolls, and calabashes of food on sticks across their shoulders. And they were bringing some of their oxen to camp meeting too. The oxen were for tithes and offerings.

When the company reached the mission, the women and children were directed to one of the shelters, and the men to the other. In the space between the shelters they built fires and cooked food. They rested, visited, and sang hymns, just as at camp meetings the world over.

All day Friday the companies kept coming. They came from all sections, singing as they came. First, very faintly, one would hear, "There's no other name like Jesus." The song would grow louder and louder, until it was broken up by welcomes and hand-shaking.

Then in a few minutes could be heard again, far-off and faint, "There is a gate that stands ajar," as another company came winding their way along the path.

So all day they kept coming, traveling one, two, or even three days' journey. No one at the mission had expected so many people. The year before, about four hundred had come to camp meeting. This year the number had doubled. They crowded the shelters. The native teachers took them to their homes in groups. The people spread their beds in the schoolrooms and filled the dispensary and workshop. Some even sought shelter in the villages near by.

Friday night the chapel was packed, and many stood outside around the windows. One after another the teachers from the various villages stood up

The schoolhouse is not big enough; two classes are meeting outdoors

and told of the wonderful things that God was doing. He had healed the sick, and had protected them in times of danger from wild beasts. Best of all, He had taken away their sins, and given them joy and gladness; and was turning the hearts of the people from their spirit worship to serve the living God. They praised God for sending them the light. A few could speak of the early days, when the pioneer missionaries had struggled with suffering and privations. Together they and the missionaries had traveled over swamp and desert. Together they had suffered from heat and cold, hunger and fever. There were times when their company had halted in a strange country far from the comforts of home, while a member was nursed and prayed back to health. They had esteemed it a privilege to ford crocodile-infested rivers that they might beg from strangers a little milk for the white child who was sick.

All day Sabbath the meetings had to be held out under the trees, for the chapel was far too small for the congregation. In the afternoon, while one of the missionaries conducted the service, the other two held meetings with the candidates for baptism. The teachers were called upon, one by one, to bring their groups of converts in for examination.

The baptism could not be held till Monday, because more time was needed to examine the candidates. In the afternoon the vast congregation gathered at the river. It was winter time, but the sun shone warm and bright, and the water was not cold.

That afternoon about sixty men, women, and children stood on the river bank awaiting their turn to be baptized. Two missionaries and two native evangelists went into the water together; thus four converts could be baptized at a time. Every year the number of baptisms doubled. Some of the students in the school rejoiced greatly to see their fathers and mothers and brothers and sisters from the home villages baptized.

As the company turned homeward, Choma walked silent and thoughtful. He was thinking of the time when he might come to camp meeting leading a band of converts. He had not seen any of his own people since he had come to the mission. He was overcome with a great longing for them.

44
Choma Visits His Home

The morning after camp meeting closed, Choma way laid his master as he was hurrying toward the school house. "Please, *m'fundisi,* I ask chance to visit my home," he said in broken English.

There was need for haste this morning, as many details were waiting to be arranged at the schoolhouse. The missionary replied without pausing: "I must attend the teachers' class now, but I will see you after breakfast."

"Please, *m'fundisi,*" Choma ran after his master, "please, the journey, very long. I wish to go part of journey with my friends. They return to their homes."

"Wait for me at the house and go on with your work."

This is a village chief such as was Choma's father, Malambo

A hurried consultation was held with the mission director; and this message was sent back to the house for Choma: "You may not go now. In two months you may go, and you will have company all the way."

So it came about that when vacation time arrived the missionary and six of his teachers went again to preach in Malambo's village; and Choma went along as cook.

The mission party were much surprised on reaching the village to see the chief men gathered together waiting to greet them. Peter explained that the news of their coming had been signaled ahead by drum beats from the last village through which they had passed.

As soon as the camp was settled, the missionary and his

teachers went to arrange for meetings with the headmen of the surrounding villages. Some of them were unfriendly and refused to allow any teaching inside their villages. Others gave the teachers a welcome. Many of the people promised to come to the camp on Sabbath.

The missionary told the company who came Sabbath morning that he had been sent by a great King to tell them of a gift that they might have without any cost. It was more valuable than any gift that any man had ever given to another. It was the gift of eternal life. But it could be had only by those who chose to turn away from sin, and to obey the King, who was God. Would they like to have the missionary and his teachers stay with them for a week, and teach them how they might obtain this precious gift? If so, would they raise their hands high?

"*Twa yanda* [we wish]," came the glad response, as all hands went up.

45
Daily Program of the Camp

During the following week, every morning at sunrise the missionary met with his teachers for prayer and Bible study. He gave them a typewritten outline of the talk that was to be given in the six villages by the six teachers that day. The same subject was presented in all the villages on the same day; then any natives who might be visiting away from their homes would not miss the topic for the day. After an hour spent together in study, the teachers retired to study and pray alone for another hour. After this they ate breakfast, and then started out in two groups of three each. At least one of the more experienced teachers went with each group. The others were student teachers.

Each group went out to three villages, and took turns preaching. Thus every teacher preached one sermon each day. Each day the teachers exchanged villages. In this way the people in each village could listen to a different speaker every day of the week. During the day, the missionary studied and prepared lessons for the opening term of school. In the evening the missionary and the teachers sat around the camp fire and talked over the experiences of the day.

On Friday the teachers announced in all the villages that there would be another union meeting at the camp on Sabbath morning. More than two hundred people came together. They sang over and over again the hymns that they had learned at the village meetings during the week.

The village people provided low stools for the missionaries and for the important men of the community. Some of the people sat on fallen logs, but most of them squatted on the ground. There were rows of young boys sitting on the ground in front. The little children sat with the women at one side. It is the rule in this country that the boys must sit and eat with their mothers until they have grown their second set of teeth. After this, they may join the group of men and big boys.

As those children lifted up their voices in song, one would have thought that they had been singing hymns all their lives. It sounded rather lusty at times, especially when slightly off tune. But to the angels of God it must have sounded sweeter than the grandest opera music.

When the missionary finished speaking, some of the teachers were called upon to give their testimony. Then Choma stood up and made his appeal. He pleaded with his own father and mother, with his brothers and sisters, with the old people and the children, to listen to the words of life. He had grown several inches in height during the three years in which he had been at the mission. His thick, black, curly hair, which stood up in a pompadour from his broad forehead, made him seem even taller than he was. His manner was quiet and dignified, and his face serious. In his clean white shirt and trousers, he looked very different from the boy who had once tied a grain sack around him and run after the mission wagon.

Before the meeting was dismissed, the missionary asked, "Will those who wish us to remain and hold meetings with you each day for another week, raise your hands?"

Once again came the response, "*Twa yanda*," as every hand was raised.

46
Choma Gives Presents

Choma's duties at the camp were usually finished early in the day, which gave the boy much leisure to spend with his own people. Once again he played with baby Luwo, who had grown to be a fine, rollicking boy.

Again he sat by his father's camp fire, not listening as in by-gone days to tales of war and adventure, but now entertaining interested groups with his descriptions of mission life, and his explanations of the Christian way. He roamed the fields with Kaluwe. He listened to Nzala's troubles. She would soon be sold to some heathen man. She wanted to become a Christian and learn at the mission school. How much Choma wished that he could take her back when he returned. But he had neither money nor cattle. He could not ransom her; and the parents were looking to the time when they might receive a good, large *lobola* (dowry, or present) for her.

The better part of his savings had been spent in buying gifts for the family. His mother's blanket had cost seven shillings. He had paid his "missis" a shilling for one of her gingham dresses. And although it was too large for Nzala and not as becoming as her buckskin skirt, Choma's heart swelled with pride at seeing her in one of the dresses which his own "missis" had worn.

Kaluwe became the happy possessor of a mouth organ that had once belonged to Oleta. Choma had parted with a precious three-penny piece to obtain it. Malambo thought his present of a slate and pencil the finest gift of all. A few pebbles in an empty cocoa tin brought screams of laughter from Luwo.

Choma gave his old primer to Milupi, with the promise to teach him how to read it. But Milupi persuaded him to exchange the primer for a worn-out watch that had fallen into Choma's possession. Milupi could see no use in learning to read the white man's books. They would not help him to grow more food or gain more cattle. But he considered the watch an attractive addition to the string of shells that he had around his arm.

While collecting presents, Choma had not forgotten the grandmother. He had begged from his missis a little bottle with a glass stopper that he had once found lying on the pantry shelf. He knew grandma would like it for a snuff case. When he learned why the mission ladies did not approve of snuff, he decided to take his grandmother a pile of memory verse cards that Oleta had given him, instead of the snuff case. But when Choma reached the home village, no grandmother was there to greet him. She had left this message,

"Tell Choma when he comes back that he must stay and teach his people about Jesus and the Christian way."

Choma wished to remain; but *m'fundisi* said he must return and finish his schooling first. Then he might come back to the village if they wanted a school. The people did want a school. They wanted one at once. More than a hundred boys and girls wanted to attend.

"We have no teachers ready to send," the missionary explained sadly. "Many, many villages are waiting for teachers. Even if our teachers were ready, they have no money or oxen with which to purchase wives. Before they go out to teach schools, they must have wives to cook for them and to care for their homes. We also need money with which to build a school for girls. Would you like to help us?"

Malambo had hundreds of cattle. He had many goats and fowls. During the past two years his crops had been good, and he was becoming prosperous. The English traders had been paying money for his corn. He had acquired quite a little pile of sovereigns and half-sovereigns. They were buried in a coffee tin under the threshold of his hut. No one but the owner knew of them at the time.

"Where can *I* find money or oxen?" Malambo asked.

"Ah!" the missionary said to his assistants, "this man has heard the gospel story, but it has not yet reached his heart."

When, after three weeks, the mission party said farewell to Malambo's village, it was with the promise that they would return as soon as possible, and that next time they came Choma would remain to open school.

On the second morning of the homeward journey, as they were preparing for breakfast, Choma introduced his brother. "*M'fundisi,* here is my brother, Kaluwe. He runs from home to go to mission. His mother refuse. He is your boy. He work for you."

This was the first time the missionary had noticed the boy. Soon after the mission party left the village, Kaluwe had gone as usual to the fields to herd cattle, and had at once struck out for the trail, leaving the cattle in the care of his mate.

All day he had followed the wagon, keeping safely out of sight. At night he had crept into the camp. Before daylight he had hidden himself again; and had then lagged behind until he thought that they were so far from home that the kind-hearted missionary would not send him back alone through that wild country. Kaluwe, too, was going to the mission.

Two Runaways

47
Queer Fears and Fancies

While Choma was growing into a noble Christian boy at the mission, a little girl named Mundea was living in a native village about three days' journey to the south. She had two younger brothers and an older sister named Setupa.

Their father was rich. He had large grain bins and many cattle. He believed that the reason for his prosperity was because he kept *tuyobela.* You never heard of *tuyobela*? Well, they are little fat men with heads and legs that turn the wrong way. So far as I have heard, they live only in the center of Africa. And they can be seen only by those who have special medicine for the eyes.

They are hard-working little fellows. Mundea's father kept ever so many of them. At night when all the family were asleep, they would sneak out in the dark and steal mealies and feed them to the children of the hut. The food, too, was never seen, and the children knew nothing about eating it because they were asleep. But this extra food made them grow strong and healthy.

Besides feeding the children, the *tuyobela* were so industrious and stole so much food that they kept their master's grain bins overflowing. But it was very risky keeping *tuyobela.*

Whenever Mundea's father went hunting, these sly little fellows would glide silently through the woods at his heels. If he was successful in killing an animal, they would be waiting to suck the creature's blood. In this way they kept themselves alive and raised the little *tuyobela.* At times, when hunting was poor, the *tuyobela* would become so hungry that they would pounce upon a living person and suck his blood.

Perhaps you have guessed by this time that all this story is only an African fairy tale, with no more truth to it than there is to some of the make-believe stories we hear in other countries. But the people of Mundea's village, as well as those living in hundreds of other villages, believe sincerely that these beings really exist, and fear them very much.

It often happened that when a person died in the village, rumor would say, "Some one in our village must be keeping *tuyobela.* They have sucked that man's blood. That is the reason why he died."

So Mundea's father was careful to guard his secret well. Not even his wife and children had any suspicion that he had these little thieves working for him. If the people had learned of this, they would have driven the family from the village and burned their house. Every one hated the *tuyobela* and anybody who kept them, for stealing their *mealies* and murdering their people.

Instead of all these queer fears and fancies, the real reason why Mundea's family always had grain in their bins was because they used so little of it in beer-making; and also because the whole family, from father and mother to the six-year old brother, worked so hard in the fields planting and digging and harvesting. This is also the reason why they were so healthy.

The women in Mundea's village bring the ears of corn back from the fields in baskets on their heads

48
Gathering and Storing Food

It was harvest time. Mundea, with her father and mother and sister and brothers, had worked early and late in the fields, planting *mealies* and kafir corn. While the grain was growing they planted peanuts and pumpkins and sweet potatoes. As soon as all the gardens were planted, while the ground was still soft from the early rains, they began clearing new lands for next year's gardens.

There was work the entire year. During the rainy season the rivers overflowed their banks, covering the lowlands. At such times the men would go to the swamps to spear fish. The women caught them in the small streams. They would make willow fish-baskets, and place them in a row across the stream. If the stream was a very wide one, they would dam it part way across, placing the fish baskets in the open space. Each basket was a trap, made in such a way that the fish could swim in, but could not get out.

Early in the morning the women would go to the river in groups. They would set their fish-baskets traps, then sit down and watch all day to see that no one stole the fish. At night they would lift the baskets of fish out of the water and carry them home on their heads. The next day they spread the fish out in the sun to dry, and afterward stored them away as relish to eat with porridge.

The grain grew fast during the short rainy season.

When it was ripe there was much work to do, gathering and storing the big, white *mealie* ears and the golden kafir corn. The women stripped the *mealie* ears from the stalks, and threw them in heaps on the ground. Rough grain bins were quickly built in the fields, where the grain could be protected from birds, mice, monkeys, and other thieves, until the women were able to transfer it in baskets to the village bins.

The grain bins were little huts built of poles and mud.

They were raised on poles about four or five feet off the ground. The roofs were woven of green twigs, covered with thatch, and placed on the bins after they were filled with grain. A little window-hole, big enough for a small boy to crawl through, was left in the wall of each bin, high up under the roof. This was carefully covered with mats.

Every morning Mundea's mother would send her out to see if the white ants were getting into the bins. These little creatures always work in the dark. They make run ways of mud up and down the poles and travel back and forth in these covered tracks. When they reach the bottom of the bin, it does not take them long to make a hole through the floor with the sharp little saws that they have in their mouths. When the owner of the bins comes to get his grain he may see only one little runway about half an inch wide leading into the bin, but inside he is likely to find that the ants have left more mud than grain.

The white ants never travel or work in the open. If their runways of mud are destroyed, they can do nothing until they stop and rebuild them. Whenever Mundea saw any of these runways leading up the legs of the mealie bins, she would scrape them off with a stick. In this way, the ants were kept so busy making new runways that they had no time to destroy the grain.

49
Intruders

One night Mundea's family were sound asleep after a hard day's work. In the middle of the night, one of the little boys gave a s ream and jumped up from his bed. This was followed by another scream from another member of the family. In half a minute all the children were hopping around screaming. Father and mother soon joined them, dancing about the middle of the hut and slapping their legs first on one side and then on the other.

The red driver ants had made them a visit. These little intruders had come like soldiers, millions of them, marching rapidly in a narrow column. They had spread themselves over the door, crawled into the beds, and then— oh, how they did bite! They buried their jaws in the flesh, and had to be pulled off with the fingers. They could not be driven off. Like a raiding army, they began to crawl over the shelves and dishes and walls, devouring everything in their track that was soft enough for them to bite into.

The little boys fanned up the fires, and their father lighted grass torches and looked around to see from which direction the ants had attacked them.

Mundea ran to the corner of the hut, where her pet hen was sitting on seven brown eggs. The ants bit her feet, but she paid little attention to them. She caught up the poor, frightened biddy in her arms, gathered the eggs into her skirt, and ran quickly to a place of safety outside the hut.

Setupa untied the goat from the shed and led her down the path in a direction away from where the ants were coming. The whole family hurried from the hut, sounding an alarm to the other villagers as they fled.

The alarm spread rapidly through the village. The sleeping people sprang from their beds, fanned up their fires, and scattered live coals and burning firebrands around the huts to make a barrier against the ants. No one in Mundea's family returned home that night. They all slept with the neighbors.

The goat fussed around for a while; but finally she went to sleep, and let the people sleep too. In the morning, the little hen went cackling back to her old home, leaving her eggs to get cold, so Mundea had to give her a new setting of eggs.

When the family returned to their hut, they found the cupboard bare and most of the food jars empty. The ants had left only the hard grain. The hut looked as clean as if it had been swept. Not a rat, nor a mouse, nor a spider, nor a cockroach, nor a fly, nor a cricket, could be found anywhere.

While the ants were cleaning out this hut, their scouts were exploring the village. But they were driven back everywhere by the walls of live coals, which were guarded all night by the village people as carefully as soldiers guard a fort. Finding no hut open to them, the ants had made a straight line out of the village, and had traveled on over the fields, murdering grasshoppers, toads, beetles, and all other living things in or near their path.

50
Setupa's Wedding

One evening while the family were sitting around the fire in their hut, the father said, "Setupa, go, fetch water; I die of thirst." Setupa went out at once to get the calabash of water that hung under the eaves of the veranda. As she was lifting it from its peg, two men pounced upon her.

She screamed and tried to get away; but the men held her fast. Her father came out of the hut, filled his mouth with water, and sprayed it over her, saying as he did so, "Now I give you to Lubinda: you are his wife."

At these words, the girl's mother came out of the hut, and helped her father to carry her inside. She rubbed fresh red paste over her body and polished her with her hands. Then she decked her in new fiber skirts, beads, bangles, and shells.

Many times the girl tried to escape, but it was impossible. The house was surrounded by men who had been sent by the bridegroom to bring her safely to him. When she was ready, they took her away, one of the men carrying her on his back. A company of her girl friends followed her.

After they had gone a little way, the girls stood still and said, "We cannot see the path." The young men who had been sent to fetch Setupa handed one of the girls a bangle, and the procession moved on.

Later they came to a stream. "We cannot cross this stream," the girls said. Again they stood still and waited for a present. This time they were given a string of beads.

By and by they stopped again. "We are tired, and can go no farther," they said, and were presented with a beautiful white shell. So they continued to find excuses for stopping and receiving presents, until finally they reached the bridegroom's home. Lubinda arose and greeted his wife. Setupa was married.

In the morning, Setupa's father's brother came for his present, and was presented with a spear. Then her mother's brother came, and received the gift of a hoe.

After this, all the bride's relatives came trooping in for their presents. They came weeping; but upon receiving their presents began to laugh and be merry. Fowls were roasted, and the wedding feast was held.

Two or three days afterward, when all the excitement was over, Lubinda sent the remaining portion of the *lobola*. He had paid a part of it before the wedding. Eleven oxen, four spears, and three hoes were the required amount, as arranged by the bridegroom's friend with the girl's father.

Setupa did not know that she was to be married until the night when the young men captured her. She was not acquainted with her husband, having seen him only a few times at a distance. But she made up her mind to be happy. She would fetch wood and water for him, cook his food, hoe his garden, and be a good wife. Following the usual native custom, Lubinda built a hut in Setupa's native village, as near to her mother's hut as possible, and he and his bride lived for one year among her people.

51
Good News

Late one afternoon, three strangers came to the village where Mundea was living. They were seeking shelter for the night. They had been working in a mine, and on their way home had stopped over night at a mission school. After the evening meal, they sat around their host's fire and talked. As they sat and talked, other people of the village gathered about to greet them and to hear their story.

They told of many wonderful things they had heard that night from the boys attending the mission school. The white teacher at the school had taught these boys about a great God who had made them. This God was good and kind, and loved His people. He pitied them, and was soon coming to save them. Even the dead would live again.

The people had always believed in some kind of a god, a great spirit, who sent them rain. The strangers sang songs that they had learned at the mission. One of them was, "Jesus loves me, this I know."

For several days after the visitors had gone on their way, the village people talked of little else except the strange news that they had brought. How could that story about the Son of God be true! No one could love them as much as that. But He had lived on the earth, and people had seen Him and talked with Him. Perhaps the story was true. They would like to know more about Him.

They had of ten wondered how people came to be living on the earth, and how there came to be an earth.

So all these things had been created by God himself! Could it be true that He would come to the earth, and make the dead to live? They would like to see the book that the white man had brought across the waters, which contained words that God had spoken.

Those who had seen the strangers were displeased with themselves for not asking more questions. Those who had not seen them were displeased with those who had for not persuading them to stay longer. Where was the school? The strangers said they had come from the north. Part of their journey had been made on the train.

What was a train? Chitumba, one of the young men, could answer that question. He had seen a train once when he went to sell oxen at the white man's village. "A train," he said, "is made of many, many sleds, fastened together, that can run along by themselves without oxen to draw them. They have wheels, and run on strips of iron. And the train makes a noise like thunder when it passes." And so, for days and weeks after that eventful night, scraps of its conversation passed from mouth to mouth, and from village to village.

52
Eavesdropping

The work of stamping the daily ration of *mealies* often fell to the lot of Mundea. The corn was poured into the stamping block (a tall bowl that had been made by hollowing out a section of tree trunk), and it was pounded with a short pole until it was ground to meal.

Mundea makes corn meal for the day's food

While busy with this task one morning, Mundea noticed a man watching her closely from a bush a short distance away. As soon as he saw that she had noticed him, he slipped away into the bushes. The next day while digging her sweet potatoes, she caught sight of him gliding among some trees near the garden.

She felt sure that the young man had been sent by her father to watch her at work, and to decide whether he would like her for his wife. Mundea did not wish to marry. She decided to keep her eyes and ears open, and to learn all she could.

One morning, shortly after this, she saw a stranger enter the hut, and sit down to talk with her father. Her mother at once called her: "Mundea, go now, and gather relish."

Mundea picked up her basket and started down the path to the fields to search for green herbs. As soon as her mother had gone inside the hut, the girl ran back quickly as if she had forgotten something.

As no one was looking, she paused under the eaves of the hut by the open window and listened. Her father was talking to the stranger. He was saying, "You know how well she works, and she is fair to look at. A man who wants a good wife will think twenty oxen a very small present to give me."

Now the stranger was talking: "My friend is a poor man. He cannot give you such a large present. Yet he wishes very much to join his family with yours, to be friends forever."

Her father began to speak again: "You have seen my daughter, and you know that she is decorated well." Mundea's chest and shoulders were marked with many little crosses. They were put on in such a way that they would never come off. Perhaps you would like to know how this had been done.

The flesh was caught up and held with small pincers while cuts about half an inch long were made in it. These cuts were arranged in groups of four, in the form of crosses. Charcoal was rubbed into the cuts to keep them from closing too quickly. When at last they did heal, Mundea's chest and shoulders were marked with the crosses, in circles like strings of beads hanging around her neck. In the eyes of these people they looked very pretty.

The visitor was speaking again: "My friend may be able to give you six oxen now, besides the ox for the mother: and five more oxen after the next harvest time."

"And the money, and the hoes?" the father was asking.

"It may be he can find a pound somewhere," the man replied.

The father gave the final answer: "He must find two pounds, twelve oxen, three spears, and five hoes. That is a very small present. My daughter is strong, and fair, and she is good-natured."

Mundea did not wait to hear anything more. She knew now that the father of the young man who had been watching her had sent his friend to arrange the *lobola*. Her father intended her to marry soon. The men would come and carry her off, as they had taken her sister. She slipped quietly away and went on her errand.

53
The Plot

Chitumba's sister, Hatuba, was Mundea's special friend. The two girls usually went to the fields together to gather relish. As Mundea passed her friend's hut, she waited outside, and gave a low call. Hatuba laid aside her work, picked up her relish basket, and went with her.

Hatuba was a little older than Mundea. The girls told each other all their daily experiences. Of late, these experiences seemed to be made up largely of troubles.

There had been a recent beer-drinking in the village. Hatuba's quick eye had seen an old man with two very long finger nails. As he passed a bowl of beer to one of the men present, she had noticed him take hold of the bowl in such a way as to put both his finger nails into the beer. The next day the man whom he had served was dead.

She suspected the old man of putting poison under his finger nails. The wizards sometimes mix up a very deadly poison from the brains of the crocodile, the roots of a very poisonous plant, a dead man's tooth, and various other horrible things.

Hatuba suspected this old man of being a wizard, and of poisoning the dead man's beer. She told her father of what she had seen. He sent a secret messenger to the British magistrate, who was making his regular tour, and was holding court in a neighboring village. The magistrate at once sent police and had the man arrested.

In the trial that followed, Hatuba was compelled to give her witness against him. Although the old wizard was now securely locked up, where he could no longer hurt any one, yet Hatuba lived in constant fear that some of his relatives would take revenge on her. She had determined to flee from the village, and had already confided her plans to Mundea.

"You have much trouble," Mundea said, as soon as the two girls were safely out of hearing. "And now I have trouble too," she added.

Hatuba's arm stole around Mundea's waist: "Tell me," she whispered.

"Father is arranging for me to marry, and I don't want to marry." Then Mundea repeated what she had overheard a few minutes before by the hut; and added, "I've decided to run away too. Let us go together. We will try to find the school of which the strangers told us. Shall we go soon?"

"Let us go tonight," Hatuba whispered. And then in a still lower voice, "My brother Chitumba told me that his path crossed the railroad when he went on the journey to sell his oxen. He will tell me the way to find it."

"When shall we start?" Mundea whispered in her friend's ear. The answer came back also in a whisper, "Tonight, after all in the village are asleep. Let us meet by the ant hill back of your *mealie* bins. When the sun is like this (Hatuba pointed toward the western sky), we will hide a calabash of meal and one of water by the path leading from the village. You can bring the meal and I will bring the water and also some nuts. We will tie the calabashes each to a stick, and hide them by the stump near the crossroads."

By the time the two girls had filled their baskets with tender herbs for relish, they had planned every detail of their flight.

54
Taking Flight

That night both the girls went to bed as usual; but neither of them slept. Mundea waited until every one in her hut was asleep. Then she gathered up her few treasures, which she had slipped under her mat before lying down, wrapped them in her skin blanket, and tied the bundle with a strip of fresh bark.

In the afternoon, while preparing for the journey, Mundea spied a snakeskin bracelet. It was filled with bits of pounded medicine roots mixed with various kinds of dried insects. The bracelet was supposed to bring good luck and many friends to the wearer. Feeling the need of it, Mundea had slipped it on her wrist.

For the tenth time, she now looked to see if the bracelet was still on her wrist, and her medicine horn hanging on its string from her neck. Reassured that her precious charms were safe, she gathered her bundle under her arm, and stepped between the beds of the other children and out of the door of the hut.

The moon was rising. This was good, for by it they would know which direction to take. She laid her bundle down against the side of the hut, and stood listening to know if any one inside was stirring.

When she was sure that no one was awake, she sped toward their meeting place. Hatuba was ready and waiting for her , with her blanket-bundle. Together they glided swiftly and silently down one of the paths leading out of the village.

At the crossroads they paused to find the sticks with the calabashes of water and food tied to them, and to fasten their bundles on the other ends. Then, balancing their sticks on their shoulders, they were away again, running as fast as they could go.

They must travel east until they reached the railroad, and then follow it north for two days. By that time they would be far enough away from home for it to be safe to inquire their way to the mission school.

There were dangers on every side. But the girls seemed to forget all of them, except one—would they be pursued and taken back to the village? They decided, however, that their chances of escape were good.

"Our people will not miss us until morning, perhaps not until time to eat," Hatuba cheerfully suggested.

"And then they will not think of our running away," added Mundea. "My mother will think that I am with you, and your mother will think you are visiting me. They will not be sure that we have run away until night, and then it will be too dark to hunt for us, and they will not know which way to go."

"Chitumba may guess where we have gone," answered Hatuba, "because I asked him many questions about the path to the railroad track. But I do not think he will tell the others, because he knows how dangerous it is for me in the village."

The girls hurried on, running for a time, then walking a little way, pausing now and then to listen to imaginary footsteps behind them. Every little noise startled them. The whir of a night hawk, or the croak of a frog; or the howling of a far-away hyena made them grasp each other's hands and listen breathlessly.

On and on they went. Their feet became sore. They stubbed their toes on stones and had to stop once in a while to remove thorns. After a delay of this kind they would run faster to make up for the time that they had lost.

Since leaving home, they had passed many villages, and were beginning to realize that they had gone a very long way. The moon was dropping toward the west. "Let us hide," said Hatuba. "In a little while the sun will shine. People will go about their work, and if we are traveling we shall be seen. The people in our village may be hunting for us today, asking in every village if two strange girls have passed this way."

Breaking away from the path, they began to look for a place in which to hide. They found a fallen tree with a thick undergrowth of bushes around it. There they dropped their burdens and sat down on the tree trunk to rest and think. They ate a few handfuls of dry grain and drank a little water from

These are grain bins like those near which Mundea and Hatuba met
before they ran from their village

their calabash. Then, by the fading light of the moon and the growing light of dawn, they gathered a few green branches and made a shelter along one side of the tree trunk. Just as it was growing light they crept under the shelter, dragging their precious bundles with them. In spite of aching feet, they were soon fast asleep.

When they awoke it was very hot. They peeked out between the sheltering branches. No one was in sight. Were they very close to a village? They lay quiet, and spoke only in whispers, so afraid were they that some passer-by might overhear them. Were they pursued? Which paths would their people be most likely to follow? Were they near the railroad? Would they know how to find it? And would they know it if they should see it?

They had heard Chitumba describe the track, with its shining rails stretching in a straight line as far as eye could see. And he had told them of the great noise, like thunder, that the train made as it passed by. All day they stayed in the shelter, sleeping most of the time. When they awoke they lay for hours whispering their plans as to how they should make the rest of the journey, and what they would do if they were caught. They listened for the great noise of the train. But they heard only the lowing of cattle, and the crack of whips as the herd boys drove them past. They must still be a long way from the railroad.

55
Dangers

Evening came on, and Hatuba and Mundea were eager to be on their way again. They crept out of their hiding place and began to look around. They did not know which way to go; and so they had to' sit down and wait for the moon to rise and show them the directions. They ate a little more grain from the calabash, but not nearly so much as they wanted. There was no way of knowing how many days their small supply would have to last. When at last they saw the smiling moon popping up out of the ground, they lost no time in getting started on their second night's tramp.

They had traveled for about three hours when, suddenly they came upon the railroad track. Turning left, they followed it to the north. Now they had a nice, straight path, with no ugly stones or thorn twigs to hurt their feet. They could not lose the way now, and felt sure of reaching safety soon.

They were in high spirits as, chattering and laughing, they tripped along the path beside the track. Every step was taking them farther from the dangers and misery of a native village. Every step was bringing them nearer to that wonderful school where they would learn about the Man who loved them so much that He had given His life to save them.

Suddenly Hatuba gave a startled cry. A few paces ahead there were two large, red eyes glaring at them from the shadows beside the path. The girls gripped each other's hands, and gasped, "A lion!"

They turned and sped backwards, wildly looking for a tree. Bushes were plentiful, but large trees were scarce in that part of the country. At last they saw one, and ran for it with all their might. Mundea sprang for the lowest branches. Hatuba pushed her up. Then Mundea pulled Hatuba up. They scrambled up and up, until they reached the highest branches.

They peered around them on every side for the red eyes; but the eyes had disappeared. In their anxiety about getting away from home neither of the girls had once thought of lions nor of leopards nor of any of the other wild beasts that were so thick in the forests, especially at night.

In a dazed fright, they clung to the branches. What should they do? It was cold. There was no human soul near to help them. They dared not travel any farther that night. And they were so tired that if they stayed any longer in the tree th y would be likely to go to sleep and fall to the ground.

At last Hatuba thought of a plan. "Mundea," she said , "you watch from the tree, and warn me if you see the eyes again." She slipped to the ground and untied the bundles, which, in their scramble, they had dropped at the foot of the tree. Then she passed the skin blankets and the bark strips with which the bundles were tied up to Mundea.

As soon as possible she scrambled up into the tree again. The girls wrapped their blankets around them, tied themselves with the bark strips securely to the branches, and slept safely in the tree all the rest of the night.

56
More Dangers

In the morning, Hatuba and Mundea went on their journey. They continued to follow the path by the rail road track. It seemed safer to them than the winding paths between the villages, because they could look far ahead, down the straight shining rails, and see travelers long before they passed them.

Once a band of hunters came along the path, with their spears over their shoulders. The girls disappeared into the tall grass, and lay down until the men had passed.

After a time Mundea stood up and looked around. "Let us go," she said; "no hunters can be seen now." Hatuba hesitated. "Come, let us go!" Mundea repeated, stooping to pick up her load.

Suddenly Hatuba sprang up, caught her by the arm, and dragged her back. A large *mamba* was drinking from her calabash of water. "He will crawl away by and by," they said. But the snake was quite content to stay where he was. He coiled himself around the calabash and prepared for a nap.

The girls became uneasy. What should they do? They had already lost much time. They were in a wild country, and knew that they should try to find

The lion was watching beside the railroad track in the moonlight

a village before night, where they might find shelter. But they were afraid to disturb the snake. The bite of the *mamba* is deadly, and the grass was tall and thick.

"We must not continue to sit here," Hatuba said; "we will be found."

"I will drive the snake away," suggested the other girl. "You watch which way it goes." She gathered a pile of stones and clods, and began from a safe distance pelting the *mamba.*

The snake reared high in the air, thrust out his tongue three or four times, and then crawled slowly and lazily away in the grass. The girls gave him plenty of time to get away. Then they picked up their burdens and hurried on, stopping only for a moment to fill their water calabash at a stream that they passed.

A little before sundown they saw a herd of cattle. The herd boys were rounding them up, getting ready to drive them home to the kraal. Unnoticed, the girls followed them to the village, where they sought shelter for the night. They were received kindly and given food. They learned that the mission that they desired to find was only half a day's journey farther on. The next morning before sunrise, they were up and away on the last stretch of the journey.

57
No Room

A little before noon, Hatuba and Mundea . trudged into the mission compound. They were taken to the director's house. He was busy in the office, and told them to wait under the orange trees. They were glad to sit and rest. The kitchen boy brought them food, which they received thankfully, for they were hungry as well as tired.

When the missionary heard what the girls wanted, he was greatly perplexed. There was no girls' compound at the mission. If harm should come to them, he would be held responsible. In a voice that showed how bad he felt, he said to them; "We have no house for you. You must go back to your home and wait for a year. By that time we hope to have money enough to build a proper place for you, and to start a girls' school."

The two girls fixed their big, frightened eyes upon him. "We cannot go back," they said.

In running away from home, they had risked capture and punishment by their parents. They had braved the dangers of strange tribes and fierce beasts in the wilderness. They had followed unknown paths into a new country to find shelter with the white man, of whom they knew so little, so that they might learn of God and of Jesus, whose name they had heard only once. It was true—*they could not go back.*

The director called Peter, and said to him, "Peter, you must explain it to the girls so they will understand. Their dialect is strange to me. Perhaps you can find some way to make them understand. Every room is full. I am sorry, but we cannot take them in now."

The girls made the same reply: "We cannot go back! *We cannot go back!"*

When the director hear their story from Peter, he called in the other two missionaries for counsel. They must help him think of some plan to care for those girls. But while they were trying to decide what to do, Peter jumped on his bicycle and rode away to his house.

When he was a young boy, he had run away from his village that he might attend the mission school. That was many years before, when the school was first started. Today, as he listened to the girls telling their story, he was reminded of the longings in his own heart, when he was a mere boy, to hear for himself the words of the living God and to learn the way of life.

When Peter returned, he went straight to the director's office. "My wife and I will take the girls," he said. "They shall be our daughters. They can help us hoe our fields and can attend the school."

Ready for Work
58
Charms

Few headmen out in the villages had as fine a hut as Peter had built for his family in the vicinity of the mission. An avenue of banana trees led up to the house. On one side of the avenue were the grain bins and various huts for fowls and farm implements. On the other side were the garden and a small orchard of young orange trees.

The hut contained three large, airy rooms. The walls of the living room were provided with numerous brackets and shelves, which had been built into the frame of the hut, and covered with the hard, white clay with which the walls were plastered. It was furnished with table, cupboard, bookcase, and several straight-back chairs, all made from packing boxes and saplings.

Stools were provided for the comfort of the children; and there was an old iron plow disk that made a foot warmer. This could be filled with burning coals, and moved from room to room. The walls of the room were ornamented with picture rolls and mottoes, and baskets containing books, slates, and trinkets.

Sara, Peter's wife, was one of the "leading ladies" at the mission. Her children were always neatly dressed, her house and yard were clean and tidy, and her *mealie* meal the finest and whitest that could be made. In spite of this, she was not too proud to go out and hoe the garden with the boys who were working for Peter and attending school.

She welcomed Hatuba and Mundea to her home and heart. And although she spoke a dialect somewhat different from theirs, they soon learned to understand one another very well. The girls willingly shared both the duties of the home and of the field.

At first they did not care for the school. They could not remember the queer little signs the teacher put on the board. Why should they have to learn them all? Surely there must be some easier way to learn to read. Could not some of their teachers provide them with magic medicine for the eyes. They made many inquiries for such eye medicine, and refused to believe that there was no such thing.

Mundea learned more readily than Hatuba. She believed that her success was due to the snake-skin bracelet that she wore on her arm, carefully hidden now under the blue calico dress that Sara had made for her.

In spite of the fact that both girls believed in charms and wore them constantly, they could not overcome their fear of being traced and pursued by the people of their home village. On their way to school, if they chanced to see strangers, they would slip away into the bush and hide until the people had passed by. When visitors came to Peter's home, the girls would run away to the fields. Once when they could not get out of the house without being seen, they hid under the bed. In no case would they consent to be seen by strangers.

Nearly half their time was spent in avoiding imaginary dangers. When in the hut at night they were careful not to look backward over their shoulders for fear of seeing their shadow on the wall; for they were sure that if they did so they would become ill.

When they combed their hair or cut their finger nails, they were careful to bury all the combings and nail clippings. If an enemy were to find these he might pronounce a curse over them, and bring harm to the one to whom they had belonged. If they found a stick lying across their pathway, they would walk around it. To step over it would bring them bad luck.

One day Sara found Hatuba sitting over a fire of bad smelling leaves that she had made for herself, inhaling the smoke. Hatuba had been worrying so much about all the terrible things that might happen to her that she was growing thin. But she thought the cause of her trouble was an evil spirit that had gotten inside of her and was devouring all the food she ate. So she was trying to drive the wicked ghost away with the bad-smelling smoke.

Day by day and week by week, Sara taught them the foolishness of fearing such things, or of trusting in charms. Jesus was their friend, and He was stronger than all the evil spirits. He had said, "All power is given unto Me in heaven and in earth." And again, "Fear thou not; for I am with thee: be not dismayed, for I am thy God." And again, "If ye shall ask anything in My name, I will do it."

There was nothing in the world they need fear, for Jesus had conquered all the evil spirits. He had all power in heaven and in earth. He was their friend, and had promised to do anything they should ask. As the girls learned to pray, they gradually lost their fears; and one after another they cast their charms aside.

59
Mapepe Dies

Choma was learning rapidly in his school work. He was now a student teacher, having been allowed to enter the teachers' class one year ahead of his grade, because of the necessity of sending him soon to open a school at Malambo's village.

Every Sabbath afternoon he took a group of students to a village about five miles from the mission, to hold gospel meetings with the people there. The little company walked all the way every Sabbath, going single file along the path, singing as they went.

Mapepe, the headman of the village, was a leper. During the meetings the poor old man sat on a low stool, away off by himself. He kept switching flies off his sores with a brush made from the tail of a zebra.

One Sabbath, when Choma had finished preaching, he went over and sat down beside the old man. He told him of God's love, and pleaded with him to give his heart to Jesus.

"No," Mapepe replied, "I cannot give up my beer. Let me go on as I am doing for two more years, then I will become a Christian."

The young teacher knelt down right there beside the poor old leper, and prayed for him. Again he pleaded, "Will you not take Jesus today? You may not live for two more years. You may not live even until we come to your village again."

But it was of no use. The old man refused to speak again. "Think of our words while we are gone," said Choma, "and give us a different answer next Sabbath." Then he turned away without saying more, sad at heart.

One day soon after this, the message was brought to the mission that Mapepe was ill. The mission director and his wife took one of the teachers and went to Mapepe's village to see what could be done to help him. But the missionaries were not allowed to enter the hut. Through the little window-hole in the wall, they could see the old man lying on his bed, wrapped in dirty rags and skins. The medicine doctor was standing over him, wildly waving two tails of animals.

When Mapepe was first taken ill, his relatives had at once sent for the witch doctor. He had come and had sat for two hours in the hut, shaking and studying his bones. Finally he had announced that a certain man wished to take Mapepe's place as headman of the village; and that for this reason he had bewitched the old man and was trying to kill him. In the olden days the accused would have been slain, but the British government now forbids any killings by the natives.

The next important thing to do was to send for the medicine doctor. He had come with his roots and powders and leaves. He had made medicine tea for the patient, and had rubbed medicine paste on his body. He had smoked the hut and the crossroads to drive off the troublesome spirits. And he had bled the old man with a little cupping horn, till he was too weak to sit up, in order to get the bad blood out.

After this the doctor had filled the two tails with his medicines, and was waving them over the patient's head when the missionaries arrived, all the while calling on the friendly spirits to help him drive away the troublesome ones. Just what kind of medicine went into those tails will probably never be known. All sorts of mixtures are used, containing such things as medicine herbs, snake's blood, dried insects, the skin of chameleons and lizards, and the ground bones of wild beasts.

When the doctor had finished waving the tails over the patient, he rushed from the hut beating the g-round to drive the spirits out of the village. He brought the medicine tails back and laid them on the bed, one on each side of the patient.

The missionary sent a picanin to call Mapepe's son. "Your father is very ill," he said. "We will care for him, if you are willing."

"My father has chosen his own doctor," the man answered, "and I dare not make any change while he is so ill." Before the week was out, the old man was dead. He had pneumonia, and there would have been little chance of saving him, even with the best of treatment.

60
The Burial Feast

A grave was dug in the yard in front of the old man's hut. He was sewed up in a fresh ox skin and buried at night by torch light. His pipe and hoe and bag of tobacco and a basket of red clay were put into the grave with him. The people said, "His spirit will need these things to use on his journey."

There was a great mourning in Mapepe's village. For three days the people daubed their faces with white clay and ashes and walked around their huts carrying spears and hoes and crying and beating their breasts.

Twenty oxen were killed, and there was feasting and beer-drinking. On the fourth day, fifty more oxen were killed, drums were beaten, and people gathered from the surrounding villages to the great feast.

The men came dressed like warriors, carrying spears. They marched about the village; and rushing furiously to the grave, they would make vicious thrusts as though spearing some imaginary enemy. This was their way of showing honor to the brave warrior and hunter who was dead. Women and children joined the procession, beating the ground with branches to drive away the evil spirits.

Finally the people washed off the old clay, and daubed their faces with fresh clay. The mourning was at an end. The people who had come from other villages returned to their homes. Only the headmen and counselors remained to decide who should take Mapepe's place. After several day's counsel, Mapepe's nephew was chosen. He was given the houses and lands and the wives and cattle that had belonged to the former headman.

When all was over, the medicine doctor came to get his present. He had promised to cure Mapepe; and Mapepe had promised to give him fifteen oxen and ten hoes. But instead of curing the patient, he had let him die. The young men of the village were angry and refused to pay the fee.

But the doctor told them that because his medicines had failed he would have to throw them all away and look for new ones. To meet this expense he demanded twenty oxen instead of fifteen. And the old people of the village, to save further trouble, insisted on giving him the twenty oxen.

Poor old Mapepe was dead. He had had many chances to become a Christian, and had refused every one. "In two years," he had said—but he died a heathen. The dances and beer drinks still continue in his village, though many of the children and young people have become Christians and no longer attend these wicked feasts.

61
Discovered

For many months after the girls disappeared, their people searched and inquired for them. No one had seen them leave the village. The witch doctors who were consulted made many guesses as to where they had gone; but their magic failed to reveal the secret. The whole village had finally given them up for lost, deciding that they must have fallen in the river, or been eaten by wild beasts.

As time went on, Hatuba and Mundea forgot their fears of pursuit. But one evening, about two years after the girls had run away, three men, carrying spears and blanket rolls, were shown into the director's office. Two of the men were the fathers of the runaway girls. The other was Chitumba, Hatuba's brother.

Chitumba believed all the time that the girls had gone to the mission school; and for that reason he said nothing to lead to their discovery. But one evening three young men from their home village stopped at the mission. They were entertained by the students with true native hospitality, that is, they were given all the *mealie* porridge they could eat, a place to sit in one of the circles by a camp fire, and a sheltered corner where they could roll up in their blankets for the night.

The next day, while watching the students line up for school, these young men had seen and recognized the two girls. When they returned home with the news that Hatuba and Mundea were at the mission, the fathers set out at once to recover their lost property. They were determined not to be cheated out of the *lobolas* which they had expected to receive for their daughters.

As soon as the men began to speak, the m1ss1onary saw that they were angry. He called for Peter, and said to him in English, "You may interpret for us. As you are well acquainted with the customs of the people, please correct any little error I may make in dealing with so important a matter. Do you think you can understand their speech?"

"I think so, *m'fundisi*," Peter replied.

The missionary smiled at the men, and said pleasantly, "You are seeking Hatuba and Mundea? We know these girls are your daughters. We have no intention of stealing them from you. Hatuba fled from danger. Mundea came with her. We have kept them safely for you. We have fed them, and clothed them, and are teaching them great wisdom.

"Two of our young men wish to marry these girls. These young men are wise and good. They will build good homes for their wives, and will clothe them well. They will be kind to them and not beat them. And they will give them one day in every week for rest. If you will allow your daughters to marry these young men, they will become great and honorable women."

The fathers replied, "Two young men in our country wish to marry our daughters. They have promised large *lobolas* for them."

"And what do your men usually give?" questioned the missionary.

"Thirty or forty oxen, and six or eight pounds," one of the men answered. The missionary knew he was not telling the truth, but was too polite to say so.

"In these parts," he said, "the people usually give about six or eight oxen, and one or two pounds."

"Our people are rich, they can pay us well. We do not wish our daughters to go away to live among strangers," the men answered.

The missionary did not know just how to deal with these men. He was thinking, and praying too, that God would teach him what to say. As he studied the matter in silence, his fingers idly tapped a glass paper-weight on his desk. Finally he said, looking at Mundea's father, "Two years ago, you arranged to take a *lobola* of twelve oxen, two pounds, three spears, and five hoes for Mundea; and you were well satisfied with that amount."

The man's lips tightened, and there was a slight flicker of an eyelash. Beyond this, he showed no sign of surprise, but he sat silent for a moment. The missionary looked at him steadily. He knew the man was wondering by what powerful magic the missionary had discovered this secret.

Mundea had told Sara the whole story of what she had heard as she listened under the eaves of her father's hut, the day of her flight from home. Sara had told Peter, and so the story had reached the missionary, who had made a careful note of the facts for future use.

When the man replied, he simply said, "My daughter is larger and stronger now."

"But she has cost you nothing since then; why should you expect to receive more for her now?" the missionary asked.

There was more conversation. Finally Peter was chosen to act as middle man, to arrange the *lobola* with the fathers of the two girls. After several *indabas,* reaching over a period of more than a week, it was arranged for Paul Choma to find ten oxen, three pounds, and five hoes for Mundea's father; and for Jeremiah Milimo, the other young man, to find twelve oxen, two pounds, and six spears for Hatuba's father.

One day, after the men had returned to their village, the mission director asked his wife, "Have you seen any thing of my paper-weight, my dear? The thing seems to have totally disappeared. Now, please tell me which one of these little heathen could possibly find use for such a thing as that?"

Peter did not want to tell tales, for fear of making trouble for one of his countrymen. But he could not bear to let the *m'fundisi* cast suspicion on any of the mission boys. At last he ventured to say. "None of the mission boys have taken the paper-weight, *m'fundisi.*"

"Then you know about this, Peter. You must tell me the truth. What do you know?"

"I have not seen any one take the paper-weight. But a man who lives at a great distance from here asked me to name for him the witch doctor who sold you the little glass that told secrets so well."

The missionary laughed, and so did Peter.

62
Finding the Lobola

As Jeremiah and Choma neared the close of their year in the teachers' class, they began to wonder where they could find money and oxen for their *lobolas*. For six years they had been working to pay board and clothes and schooling. During the past year, since their marriage had been arranged they had been given a garden plot to work for themselves after the regular working hours. At the end of the season they were able to sell a few bags of corn to the mission.

Although Peter had done his very best in arranging the *lobolas* with the fathers of Hatuba and Mundea, the amount was much larger than the young men could hope to pay themselves. The two young men had about one fourth the amount saved up. They could not ask help of their fathers, because the fathers had chosen heathen girls for their sons to marry.

But the young men were determined that they would never do this. They had seen the trouble that had come to some of the other Christian teachers who had married heathen women. Their wives were often too lazy and untidy to keep their huts clean. Sometimes they were spiteful because their husbands refused to join in the drunken dances of the village, and would cut their blankets and put sand in their food.

While Choma was studying over the matter, he received a letter from Tito, one of his classmates. Tito was a bright boy. The missionaries had planned that he should open a school in the vicinity of the mission the following term.

One day Tito had come to the *m'fundisi*. "I wish to go to my home to attend the burying of my uncle." He had promised to return in four weeks. Nearly a half year had passed, and he had not come back.

Choma kept Tito's letter in his pocket for several days. Then, one day after school, he told his *m'fundisi* about it. "Will you read me the letter?" the missionary asked. Choma read the letter, translating it into English as he read:

"To my friend Paul Choma:

"I write to ask about your life. Myself, I am healthy. For five months now, I am work at Bulawayo here for painter. My wage, it is two pounds for every month. My money is now eight pounds, three shillings. I have fifteen shillings, no more, when I arrive at Bulawayo. Now, because I write is this; the missis here wants very much a house boy. She make promise thirty shilling for good boy. Come yourself—the work it waits. It is good position.

"Your friend,

"Tito."

"What are you going to do about it?" the missionary asked.

"I cannot say," Choma replied. "Where can I find my present for my wife?"

"You mean the *lobola?*"

"Yes, I have not so much money."

It was a hard question for the missionary to answer. There were no funds in the mission treasury to use for such a purpose. This difficulty over the *lobola* had delayed many teachers from going out to their schools. The boys who went to the towns and took positions as house boys in order to earn the necessary cash often fell under the temptation of money, and never returned to the mission. It was hard to take up teaching for fifteen shillings or a pound a month after they had been earning two or three pounds.

The mission was poor. During the past year, there had not been enough food because of poor crops, due to late rains and short planting seasons. The school had been forced to cut down and send thirty of the boys home.

The mission director and his wife had taken sixty pounds of their own money, all they had in the world, and had spent it for corn to feed the students, in order that the school might not have to be closed altogether.

In humility, the missionary bowed his head. "Choma," he said, "I think we should pray to God. We have done all that we can do. God owns the whole world. He can help us. The people in your village have waited long for a teacher. Must they wait longer while you earn this money, or shall we ask God to send it?"

So right there the pupil and his teacher knelt together in the little mission chapel, and asked God to help them get the money that they needed for the *lobola.* Choma refused to leave the mission. He wrote and told Tito why he could not accept the position.

A few days after this, the post boy brought the missionary a letter containing one hundred dollars. It had traveled many thousands of miles. This money had not been asked for. It came as a great surprise. The friend who sent it said: "Please use this money to put new thatch on your house, to replace those veranda posts that you said the ants had eaten, and to buy new screen that will keep out the mosquitoes. If there is any money left after this has been done, use it as you think best."

Oleta and her mother were called to share the good news. There was great rejoicing. "Now we can keep out those horrid mosquitoes," mother said. "I killed about two hundred of them on the inside of the screen last night."

"And we'll build that extension to the veranda on the cool side of the house," added daddy, "and put on thatch a foot deep. Then there'll be no more hot, sleepless nights for you, my dear."

Then an idea seemed to strike them both at the same time—was this the money they had been praying for to help Jeremiah and Choma pay their *lobolas?* The fever season was over for the year; money for the new pillars and screen might come before another year. And there weren't very many hot nights in one summer.

But what would the friend think who sent the money? "If he could be with us, he would understand," said daddy. "If he could himself hear the cry *'Twa yanda* [we want]! We want Christian teachers! We want to find the way of life! We want Jesus!'—if he could hear that cry going up from these hundreds of villages, he would be glad to have us use this money to help these young men. If God's people everywhere could hear this cry going up from Africa, from all the world, they would care very little for comfort or luxury."

The cattle and money were sent to the fathers of the two girls. Choma and Jeremiah promised that when they become prosperous, and owned cattle and *mealie* fields of their own, they would return this loan of money to the mission so that it might be used to help other young men who were in the same difficulty in which they had been.

63
A Christian Wedding

Camp meeting followed the closing days of school. It was the largest camp meeting ever held on the mission and there were two hundred and forty converts. Mundea and Hatuba were to be baptized. They went into the water hand in hand. They were beautiful in their white dresses and turbans. Peter baptized them. Two missionaries and three native evangelists were baptizing, and five people could be baptized at once. The company of people on the bank were singing, "I will follow Thee, my Saviour" as the two girls with their three companions came up out of the water. It was a day of great joy.

The next day a special announcement was made. All the school boys were to be excused from their after noon's work that they might attend the wedding of Paul Choma and Jeremiah Milimo.

The little mission chapel had been decorated with green boughs. There was a row of potted ferns and geraniums along the platform. The brides, Hatuba and Mundea, were coming from Peter's house, which had been their home for two happy years.

All night they had cried—it was the custom to show sorrow at leaving their homes. But now, like merry children, they came tripping and skipping and singing with their girl companions.

Mundea and Hatuba, with a procession of their friends,
on the way to the chapel to be married

Oleta saw them coming. She ran quickly, joined the company, and came skipping in with them. The brides wore white dresses and veils, and carried large bouquets of wild flowers. Choma and Milimo wore white shirts and trousers.

Peter stood up to give the brides away. Oleta's father read a passage from the Bible, the mission director described a Christian home, the brides and grooms repeated their marriage vows, then all knelt in prayer. It was a real Christian wedding, very different from the heathen marriages.

There was special music by various teachers and students. Then followed congratulations. After the ceremony, trays of johnny-cake and baskets of oranges were passed among the students. Then the brides and grooms went over to the director's house to see their wedding presents.

The whole mission family felt thankful to God that these two young men had found good Christian wives. But the workers kept on praying and hoping that they might have a girls' school, where Christian women could be trained, as Ha tuba and Mundea had been, to help in the great work before them.

64
Ready for Work

Choma and Mundea were ready now to begin their life work. They would begin by starting a school in Malambo's village. Choma had been at the mission six years, Mundea only a little more than two. Although she had not learned English, she could read well in her own language. She knew how to keep house, and sew, and care for the sick. She could tell Bible stories as well as Choma, and she knew the power of Jesus to rid her heart of sin and fear.

Two days after the wedding they were to start on their journey. The small wagon that had taken the mission family on their first visit to the village was loaded with the few pots and household goods that Choma had acquired, and food enough to last until they could plant a garden and raise *mealies* for themselves. Slates and charts, a few books, and a blackboard were also taken.

The night before they were to leave, the two young folks came to say good-by. Choma knew that the missionary, too, would soon be going away, and would be selling some of his books. "I wish to buy a few books," he said.

"Do you see any that you want?" the missionary asked.

Choma made his selection. The missionary took them from the bookcase and stacked them on the table. Choma proudly drew out of his pocket six shillings. "How much cost of these?" he asked.

"Very much money," replied the missionary.

"How much?" persisted Choma.

The missionary made a rough calculation.

"More than three pounds, Choma," he finally answered. He did not dare to say how much more.

Here is the boy's dormitory at the mission, and the wagon drawn by twelve oxen in which Choma went to start his school

Choma could not hide his disappointment. "I have only six shillings. Would *m'fundisi* let me have the books now to read? I need very much. I will sent money to the America for you."

"You may have this book for six shillings, and these others are a present to you and Mundea from your *m'fundisi* and the missis," and the precious books were placed in the young man's arms.

"When you go to the America, will you find books that are more cheap for your people at the mission here?"

"I will try," was the reply. "And now let us kneel and pray that God may bless you and your school." After listening to a few final instructions in regard to returning the wagon to the mission at once for the missionary to use on another trip, the young people bade the family good-by.

Oleta and her mother were going with daddy to hold meetings in a new village, where Jeremiah and Hatuba were going to live and open a school. It would be their last village trip together for a long, long time. The thought made them sad. But the joyous anticipation of seeing their own dear children and other relatives and friends from whom they had long been separated, soon drove all thoughts of sadness away.

Oleta was going with her father and mother on a big steamer to visit their own country. Wallie and Toots and little brother had already gone with their father and mother far to the north to open a new mission. They were living among tribes who still secretly murder people for witchcraft, and throw unlucky babies to the crocodiles.

Teddy and Baby Rose were still quite well, in spite of their travels among the African villages. Teddy had lost his eyes, and had some new ones that were made of shoe buttons. However, he seemed to be able to use them just as well as he did the others. Baby Rose had been in the sanitarium several times with loose joints; and once, when her scalp fell off, she had had to go to the hospital. But she had made a good recovery, and was as spry as ever.

But Betsy Bobbit, who had had such an easy life, had quite gone to pieces. First the pink come off her cheeks. Then she got so thin she could scarcely stand up leaning against the wall. And finally, her head cracked and fell off of itself, and she died of old age before she was seven years old.

"A bad case of nerves," daddy said, "brought on by sitting around the house and taking care of herself." But mother insisted that it was all her fault, because she told Oleta that Betsy was too frail to bear the hardships of the outschool trips. Probably she couldn't have stood it long, but she would have had a useful life. And this would have been a comforting thought now that she was gone.

65
Building the Schoolhouse

When the wagon came back from Choma's village, daddy and mother and Oleta went in it to the village where they were to make their last visit before going away.

Before the meetings were over, the headmen of the vicinity met together, selected a site for their school, and then walked forty miles to the government county seat, to ask permission from the magistrate to open the school.

Daddy had a happy surprise for Oleta. He had decided that there was sufficient time to swing around by Malambo's village on their way home. Once more she could see her dear friends, Choma and Mundea.

When they reached Malambo's village, they found the schoolhouse nearly built. The walls were finished and ready for plastering. Choma told them just what had been done. As soon as they arrived in the village, Choma had sent some big boys with axes to cut poles in the forest. He gave the smaller boys sharp knives, and told them to cut strips of bark from the trees. The women and girls gathered the grass for thatching.

When all the materials were ready, the work of building began. Trenches were dug for the walls of the school house. The poles were placed on end, side by side in the trenches, and fastened 'with the bark strips to horizontal poles.

During the hot part of the day, Choma taught school under a tree. When the frame of the school was finished, it was left for a few days to give the poles time to dry. The work of building was stopped for a time, but school went on every day. The blackboard and chart were hung up on a tree. Choma told the Bible stories from the picture rolls, and the pupils were taught how to sing the hymns. As soon as a boy had mastered a page in the reading chart, he was sent with a group of boys to form a new class under another tree. Before the building was half finished the school was in full swing.

The very day before the missionaries arrived, Choma had made this announcement: "Tomorrow there will be no school. We will have a bee instead. All those who wish to continue in the school must come and help plaster the schoolhouse. Bring all the shovels and hoes you can find, and bring waterpots for carrying water."

The visitors were glad they had arrived in time for the bee. The first thing the men did in the morning was to dig a wide pit in the ground. They threw out the dirt and gravel until they reached the smooth clay. This they piled up

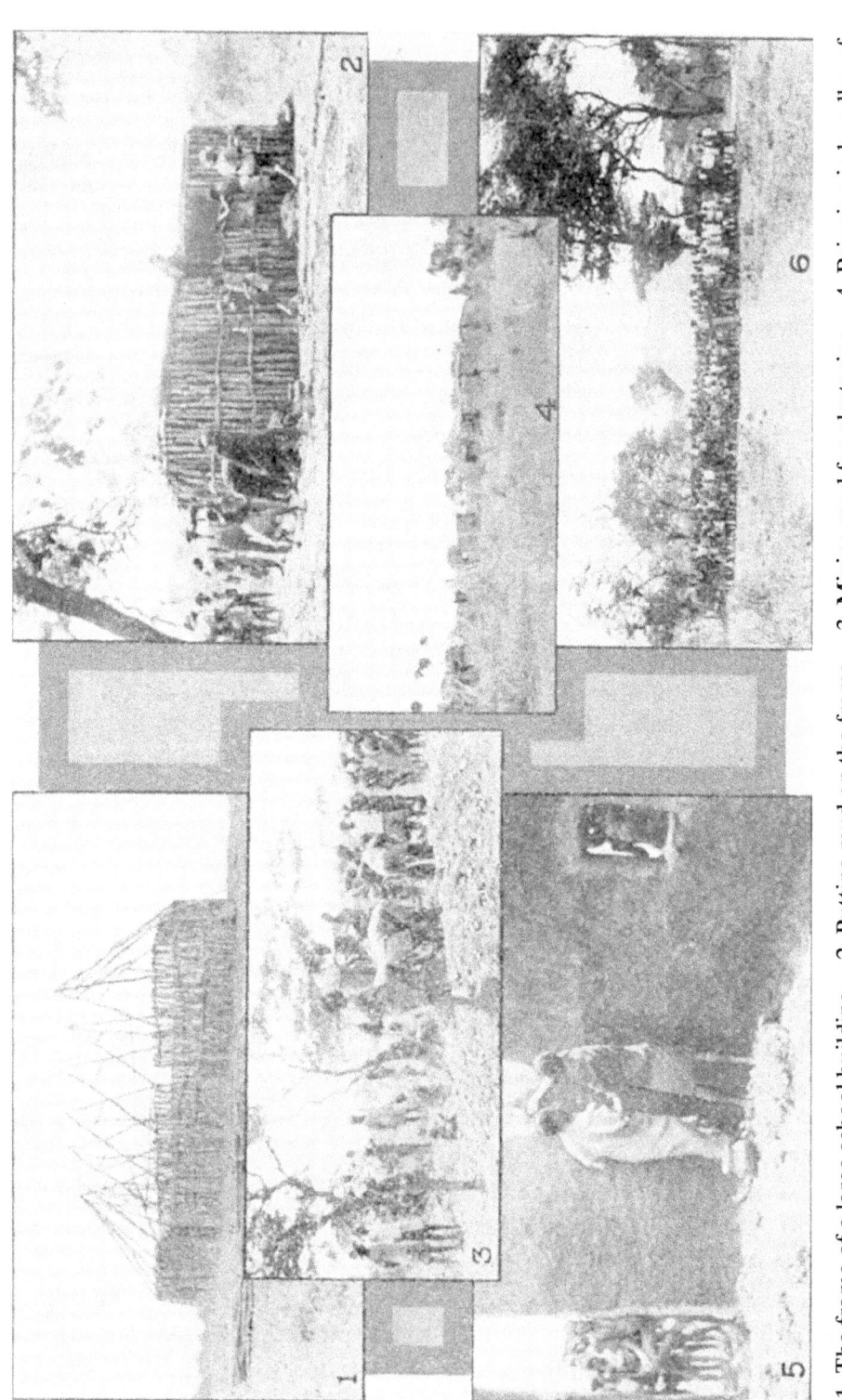

1. The frame of a large school building. 2. Putting mud on the frame. 3. Mixing mud for plastering. 4. Bringing in bundles of grass. 5. Plasterers smoothing the walls with their wet hands. 6. The congregation on Sabbath.

at the side of the pit. While the men and boys were getting the clay ready, the women and girls were fetching water from the river.

The water was poured over the clay, and the men kneaded it soft with their feet. Then they rolled it into balls which were given to small boys, who carried them to the schoolhouse. The plasterer would pick up a double handful of mud and throw it against the wall with such force that it was driven into the cracks between the poles. Then he smoothed it over, first with a flat piece of wood, and then with his wet hands.

After the plastering was finished inside and out, the dirt floor was covered with moist clay, and tamped down hard and smooth.

While the work was going on, Mundea built a camp fire and cooked big pots of porridge. She sent little girls to gather baskets of wild fruit. The food was distributed among the workers in order that they might not have to go home to eat. Choma feared that if they went home for food they might not return again to finish the plastering.

Oleta wished very much to stay arid see the school house finished. But daddy said that would be impossible, for they might miss the train that was to take them to the boat.

So Choma explained to them how the building would be finished. As soon as the walls were dry, a roof of poles would be built over the building. They would weave tender branches in and out among the poles, fastening them all securely together with bark strips.

The next thing to be done was to sew on the thatch with a needle and thread. Choma sent a picanin to fetch a needle, so Oleta could see it. The needle was made of wood, and was about a foot long. The eye had been burnt in with a red-hot poker. Fresh bark strips served for thread.

Then they all went with Choma to watch two men who were sewing the thatch on their roof. One man was on the roof, and another was standing on a platform inside the hut. The wooden needle was passed back and forth from one to the other through the roof, until all the grass was securely fastened in place. This work required several days.

Choma brought his sister Nzala to see Oleta and her mother. Nzala had a baby boy of her own now, but she attended the school under the trees, along with the boys and girls of the village. Little Luwo was the youngest member of the class. The oldest one was a woman of sixty years. Choma's father and mother did not come to school, but they both attended the baptismal class.

66
One More Gleam of Light

The baptismal class numbered two hundred and eighteen. On Sabbaths, many people came from the villages around. Those living far away would leave their homes early in the morning, bringing food with them so that they could stay all day and attend the meetings.

Many of the people had already stopped drinking beer and smoking. Choma had promised to teach his people how to plow with oxen. Then they could get better crops, there would not be so much hunger in the villages, and the women and children would not have to work so hard in the fields. He would show them how to dig deep wells, to prevent there being so much sickness from bad water. He would teach them how to read the word of God for themselves.

Mundea would show the mothers how to make dresses for themselves and their children; and how to care for cuts and bruises to keep them from growing into ugly sores.

Together they would live the gospel, caring for the sick, and showing the people how to live good, pure, Christian lives. They would form a Sabbath school and m1ss1onary society. In time the young people would learn to go out to the surrounding villages with song books and picture rolls, telling the simple Bible stories they learned in the school. The boys and girls would carry wood and water for the old women, and visit the sick.

On the morrow the missionaries must go. Choma and Mundea, who only a few years before had never heard of God except as *Leza,* the rain god, would be left alone with this great work, encouraged now and then by visits of native evangelists or the missionaries on the station. One more gleam of light had flashed out amid the darkness of heathenism.

When Choma said good-bye for this last time to Oleta, he gave her a letter to take to the boys and girls in her own country. He could not express his thoughts as well in English as in his own language. But here is the letter just as he wrote it:

"Dear Brothers and Sisters:

"We thank God that He send us the light. These tithes that you send us, they help to buy books and to give teachers for us.

"Now gospel is going to every world. We were dancing, drinking beer, and smoking pipe. Now this time we leave all this wrong way to follow the light.

"Over there," this man says, "is my village, where no missionary has ever been, nor any Christian teacher"

"Always in our prayers we ask for you that you may not be weary to help us. You cannot think how our people they are in the darkness still.

"May God bless you until Jesus He come.

"Your brother,

"Paul Choma."

When at sunrise the next morning the mission wagon rolled out of the village, Choma and Mundea remained behind. Oleta watched them, as they stood on an ant hill waving their bandanas, until they became tiny specks of black against the glowing eastern skies. And then, because she was still just a little girl, she laid her head in mother's lap and cried.

We invite you to view the complete
selection of titles we publish at:

www.TEACHServices.com

Scan with your mobile
device to go directly
to our website.

Please write or email us your praises, reactions, or
thoughts about this or any other book we publish at:

P.O. Box 954
Ringgold, GA 30736

info@TEACHServices.com

TEACH Services, Inc., titles may be purchased in bulk for educational,
business, fund-raising, or sales promotional use.
For information, please e-mail:

BulkSales@TEACHServices.com

Finally, if you are interested in seeing
your own book in print, please contact us at

publishing@TEACHServices.com

We would be happy to review your manuscript for free.

www.ingramcontent.com/pod-product-compliance
Lightning Source LLC
Chambersburg PA
CBHW081922170426

43200CB00014B/2801